The Fall of the House of Windsor

Can the Firm endure?

By Nicholas Kollerstrom

ISBN   9781739999490

Other books by the author:

Terror on the Tube, Behind the Veil of 7/7 – an Investigation 2012

How Britain Initiated both World Wars 2017

False flags over Europe – A Modern history of State-Fabricated Terror 2018

The Great British Skripal Hoax 2018

Who did 9/11? A view from across the Pond 2019

The Novichok Chronicles 2021

Acknowledgement: thanks to image libraries 'shutterstock.com' and 'commons.wikimedia.org' for use of images. Thanks to Stephen Windsor-Clive for guidance and advice.

Contents

Chronology

1999		Charles at 80th birthday of Jimmy Savile

1999   Charles at 80th birthday of Jimmy Savile

2011 Oct.   Funeral of Jimmy Savile, Charles & Camilla lead tributes

2021 April   Prince Philip dies

2022 June   Platinum Jubilee celebrations for queen's 70 year reign.

        August: 25th anniversary of Diana death

        Sept.   Queen dies, Britain's longest serving monarch.

                   => Charles king

2023 May   Coronation, Meghan Markle stays away

2024 January   Sarah Ferguson diagnosed with cancer

        Feb. 5th   King receiving cancer treatment announced

        Feb 25th   Thomas Kingston found dead, gun nearby

        Mar. 18th Palace announces that Charles is not dead

        June   The King's head goes onto UK currency.

                   Anne 'hit by horse,' loses memory

Andrew

2000   April   Andrew becomes close to Ghislaine Maxwell

2006   July   Jeffrey Epstein at birthday of Andrew's daughter Beatrice.

2011   July   Andrew to stand down as British trade envoy

2019   Nov.   Andrew's BBC interview => exit from royal life.

2022   Feb.   Queen pays £12 million to Virginia Guiffre, for Andrew.

Kate & William

2011 April   Kate & William marry

2013 Dec 2-6   Kate in hospital, her pregnancy announced

June   Kate attends Trooping of the colour, clearly not pregnant.

July 22 Birth by Kate of 'Prince George,' alleged.

2023 June   Middleton family business goes broke, owes £2 million,

Dec. 25 Last sighting of Kate.

Dec 28 Ambulance escorted by police cars leaves Sandringham

2024 Jan. 9th Kate's 42nd birthday – No party, no birthday wishes.

17th Palace announces Kate underwent abdominal surgery

18th William visits Kate at King Edward VII hospital.

28th Spanish journalist: Kate in a medically-induced coma.

29th Kate supposedly returns to Windsor castle .

Feb. 1st Revealed: her family were not told about operation.

25th Thomas Kingston killed

27th William pulls out from King Constantine memorial

March 5th 1st fake picture of Kate released, with mother in a car.

5th British Army removes a post about Kate event, June 8th

6th Kate's uncle Gary Goldsmith asked, 'where's Kate?'

10th Mother's Day second fake pic of 'Kate' with happy kids.

11th 'Kate' issues apology for fake pic + a new one appears.

16th 'Kate' seen in public with "William' at farm shop.

18th Video appears, of a tall, young girl with 'William' at farm.

20th Getty Images: a picture of Queen had been photoshopped

22nd An AI simulation of Kate on a park bench, says has cancer.

April 23rd Photo of Prince Louis on his 6th birthday.

June 15 'Kate' reappears at Trooping of the Colour

July 13 'Kate' at Wimbledon tennis final

Oct. 10 Kate reappears in public.

Harry & Meghan

2013 August Meghan divorces her 1st husband Trevor

2017 Sept.   Meghan's last scene from *Suits*, the cable TV show.

2018 May   Harry & Meghan married, in chapel at Windsor Castle

October Meghan announces pregnancy at Eugenie's wedding

2019 May 6 Meghan allegedly gives birth to Archie at Portland Hospital

2019 Dec.   H & M 'relocate' to Canada, avoid Xmas with Royals

2020 January Queen strips Harry of HRH title – he's just a prince.

June   'Mexit,' the couple move to California

2021 March   The Oprah interview, H&M denounce Royal family

June 4th Harry & Meghan child Lilibet born, allegedly.

2022 Feb 6th Harry flies from LA to London, sees Charles for 12 minutes.

Dec.   The 'Netflix series

2023 January Harry's *Spare* is world's No. 1 bestseller

March   Harry & Meghan evicted from the royal Frogmore cottage

2024 February Harry loses Court case, must pay £½ m. court costs.

April   Harry renounces British citizenship

June   Harry evicted from the Invictus games

The Saxe-Coburg dynasty

Queen Victoria & Albert Saxe-Coburg

Edward VII 1901-1910 * George V 1910- 1936 * Edward VIII 1936   *
George VI 1936-52 * Elizabeth II 1952-2022 * Charles III 2022

1

Did AI Simulate a Princess?

A thousand-year-old crown. These days Britain spends several hundred million pounds a year in maintaining it.[1] Could it be coming to an end, in our time? Its popularity and perceived relevance have descended to record low levels, with millennials now favouring its abolition. It all worked while the old Queen was alive, and the army pledged loyalty to her. There was a certain mystique, a decorum, a sense of propriety, that was necessary for its endurance, which has now vanished. The vanished glory of the English Crown reflects the psychic dissolution of the British people.

The Queen's Head remains on the currency more than two years after her death. Is this due to fears of the King's imminent demise, or is it just that no-one really wants Charles' head on the notes. Serious considerations as regards the stability and credibility of the pound sterling may arise in this regard.

* The Princess, future Queen of England, vanished mysteriously for between eight to ten months, during which she was *simulated* by a sequence of fake videos, c.g.i. etc: nobody is about to tell you who made them. That did somewhat stress and demoralise the British people and was that intentional? Speaking personally, I was impressed by the way her simulated voice – from the AI entity sitting on the park bench in March of 2024 - did synchronise quite well with her lip movements. Other things were less impressive however, e.g. the way her ring – Diana's ring! - would appear and disappear as her hands moved. Hands are difficult for AI to simulate. The vertical bench slats were of different sizes on each side of the Princess. She just had a rather obvious 'green screen' behind her on which not a blade of grass moved. In retrospect we the public have never been given any scrap of evidence that she had cancer, as averred.

---

[1] The republic.org.uk estimates £345m p.a.

Did AI Simulate a Princess?

We'll see how respect for the Crown was greatly undermined by Ms Markle and her captive Harry in recent years. The King decreed in the spring of 2024 that Harry and Meghan would be welcome to Balmoral in the summer of 2024, BUT they would have to bring their two children. Would that be a problem, or why would the king have requested that? Royal experts were coming to suspect that those two youngsters may not exist. They became fed up with the bluff, which has involved the borrowing of other people's children and at times the carrying of a rubber doll. How long will the British media endure this bluff?

Figure: The Queen waves farewell

These are the issues we will be covering, and they involve the dual themes of *unreality* and *illusion*. Charles waits all his life – seventy years – to be king, then gets sick upon receiving the crown. Should Lady Di's advice have been taken? In her *Panorama* interview, Our Princess, the Queen of Hearts - bumped off because she was too much loved by the British people[2] - stated that the crown should pass straight to William, by-passing Charles. Charles has some fine qualities (cough, cough), having helped to inspire and nurture business enterprises around the world, but may not be that suitable for wearing the Crown. Part of the mystique of monarchy in this modern age involves keeping one's mouth shut and not expressing political opinions. The old Queen was always able to do that. Also she could be mild,

---

[2] See Appendix. John Morgan, *The Assassination of Princess Diana*, 2012.

in expressing friendship towards Commonwealth countries, that sort of thing.

A hundred million was spent on Charles' Coronation, together with his ultra-ugly wife Camilla as the Queen consort. Only the Brits can still remember how to do all the pomp and ceremony with the costumes and lovely horses etc, but what a shame there is no trace of wisdom behind this facade, of this now-fading institution. A central purpose of monarchy should be to set an example to people and help the arts to flourish by keeping the nation out of wars whereas the House of Windsor rubber-stamps every conflict the British army is drawn into, as well as promoting arms sales to many countries. Thus, King Charles has given a speech supporting Israel in the current conflict.[3] He has always needed to hold forth with his opinions. Had the Crown passed straight to William as Lady Di advocated then the essential mystique of the English crown might well have endured.

[Note for persons not familiar with royal etiquette: Camilla isn't the Queen as such, only queen consort, because she is Charles' second wife. Upon Charles' passing, she won't remain queen. She is not in herself a queen.]

William is royal. His father is, we venture to presume, the King of England and his mother was Lady Di, Our Princess, whose royal lineage was quite as good as Charles', in fact better in terms of its English descent. It's hard to imagine the level of trauma he experiences, with a mother brutally murdered and he's not allowed to talk about it – or even enquire who did it, with shadowy possibilities that the Crown itself was involved. As regards his wife vanishing from public view for six months, let's hope the stories about his violent temper are untrue and that the ambulance and police escort which left Sandringham on 28 December, 2023, presumably carrying Kate, were not in consequence of his actions. Kate was a decent glamour image of royalty, ever holding her vacuous smile. It wasn't her fault if she could not get pregnant. Instead, William had to express his seed into a test-

---

[3]   expose-news.com/2023/11/07/king-charles-has-no-pretence-of-neutrality-he-supports-israel/
expose-news.com/2024/03/06/the-united-kingdom-zionisms-covert-nerve-center/

tube. Ah, what one does for England! As long as no-one asks him about these things he may be able to cope.

Figure: was it true love?

Whereas, Harry can't, he is always going to be a greviously damaged human being. He knows perfectly well who his father is and it's not Charles. For him, the pain won't go away. Maybe therapy could heal even so deep a condition, BUT only if one is able to talk about it, and do so with some degree of honesty. That is not an option for Harry – like William he can't talk about who bumped off his Mother, though he may dimly sense, now and then, that British intelligence was involved: plus he can no longer manage to see his father James Hewitt – as he used to; just occasionally and covertly. Both his book *Spare* and Hewitt's book have stated categorically that Hewitt's affair with Di only began a year after he was born: reminding one of the Journalist's motto, 'Never believe anything until it has been officially denied.'[4]

Harry did cause considerable pain to the royals by that Oprah interview, insulting them as the aged Prince Philip lay dying. And then he caused further insult by releasing his book *Spare* in the last months of the Queen's life. He then caused further insult by stealing the personal, private term of endearment for the Queen – 'Lilibet' (a contraction of 'Elizabeth') towards the end of her life, plainly without her consent – only Prince Philip had used this term of endearment towards her, once all her earlier family had gone

---

[4] Quoting from *Spare*, "Pa liked telling stories, and this was one of the best in his repertoire. He'd always end with a burst of philosophizing, 'Who knows if I'm really the Prince of Wales? Who knows if I'm even your real father?'"

Did AI Simulate a Princess?

[As a child growing up, Diana would allude to the queen as 'aunt Lilibet.' Her father Earl Spencer was then the Queen's equerry and they lived near Sandringham]. Harry used that name for his second child – one that doesn't even exist!

Harry then claimed to be outraged and distressed when Charles denied him further use of Frogmore Cottage, a royal residence. In 2020 the Queen stripped him of the title, His Royal highness, which one may compare with her stripping Prince Andrew of his royal titles – one of her last acts, towards her favourite son – in 2022. Harry is a fine public figure and being a son of Diana has got some sterling qualities – energy, action and good looks. He'll never read a book, and let's not imagine he actually wrote *Spare*. His future is unclear beyond promoting his wife's strawberry jam. He used to be promoting the *Invictus* games for handicapped people. Is he an American or a UK citizen? He says he's thinking about becoming a US citizen, but he may not be in a hurry because of all the tax on his overseas investments he'd have to pay.

The British monarchy maybe could have averted its present dismal course had the two brothers been emotionally able to support each other. They look so fine together. Neither look remotely like Charles but let's not go into that. There's a lot they could have said to each other, by way of support during the nightmare they have and still are experiencing. One may however endorse William's position of refusing to speak to his brother, after the malevolence expressed by Harry towards the Royal family. Here we note a very central quote that Harry would often come out with: 'If you knew the things that I know, you would understand that this is the only choice.' Whatever this is alluding to, he could have shared it with William.

Do either of them have *virtue?* For royalty that does have a primary meaning, in terms of providing an heir to the throne. *Neither have done that.* The law of the land here is quite definite, that an heir to the Crown, to be in the line of succession, has to have come from the body of the Mother with the birth clearly witnessed. Neither of the two wives wanted to spoil their photograph-able figures by going through motherhood. That could be a reason why Kate was disposable? Just a thought: not having provided legitimate heirs, but only the simulation thereof. But perhaps that is all that matters these days.

Did AI Simulate a Princess?

Do you know a single pop song that endorses motherhood? Have you ever in your life heard one? No? Maybe royalty expresses popular sentiment in this regard. Somewhere, hidden, is the surrogate mother. The two wives have nothing much to say that you'd want to hear, and so by their figures they were and are judged. Maybe Kate's slim, boyish hips could never have given birth. A couple of bent doctors seem to have been enough, they signed the birth-certificate.

> <u>Quiz Question about the Absence of our Future Queen</u> – Can you pick the right answer?
>
> 1. A clone of Kate Middleton is being grown, which takes six months
>
> 2. A Kate Middleton Mark II is being shipped over from *Alpha Centauri*, but it will take a while to arrive
>
> 3. Her heart was ripped out and eaten by high-ranking satanists, just as they did with lady Di.
>
> 4. She'll soon be better and her beaming face will reappear in the glossy mags.
>
> 5. Kate is a male tranny, shown by her small, manly hips, who has now abandoned her female persona.
>
> Yes, you guessed correctly, it was No. 4! … or was it? In Chapter 8 we ponder this matter.

Here in the meantime is a quote from Meghan:

We're only one plane crash away from the throne!

She has been so successful in what she has done so far, who dares put a limit? Years older than Harry, 43% Nigerian (NB, no-one believes this, whatever it is supposed to mean) and 5'5" high, she has produced what we have been shown as two marble-white kids, with ginger hair. With Harry and Meghan ruling this country … we'd have a republic in no time.

We've now looked at what will be the main themes, and this book becomes null and void if any of them can be refuted:

- Harry is the son of James Hewitt
- The Princess Kate Middleton vanished for at least eight months in 2024, during which Britons were deceived by doubles, photoshop forgeries and, worst of all, by an AI simulation. Where was she?

6

- Neither of Di's two sons have produced legitimate heirs to the throne, because their wives have not been pregnant: William has surrogate or test-tube babies, which means he may not be sure that they are his, Harry has two make-believe kids.

Those are our core themes. Feel free to slam the book down in rage … and then, read on.

Kate loved the Wimbledon tennis championships, where she used to give out the prizes. Thin and frail, did she turn up on the last day, July 15th?

The point is, I suggest, that people do not normally vanish from public view when diagnosed with cancer, it's just not that sort of illness. Thus our late Queen battled with bone cancer for a couple of years before her death, (disclosed in memoir by Boris Johnson) but that never stopped her from appearing in public.

I should perhaps apologise for including a who-did-it account of the violent murder of Our Princess, our Queen of Hearts, back in 1997. That could be the part which readers will find hardest to accept. Why, have we not heard enough about that, the reader may exclaim? Can we not forget about it, as being yesterday's news? We have certainly heard more than enough obfuscation of the case. Official lies began to emerge mere hours after the event, whereas the truth took fifteen years to emerge – yes, that is the world we live in.

That darkly transformative event lurks as a kind of unexploded bomb behind the main history we recount here. As such it is highly relevant in terms of the psychic instability of the two sons. Harry's book states that the pursuing paparazzi are to blame and is he really dim enough to believe that? Or, will Diana's two children gradually come to understand who killed their mother and why?

2

The Enveloping Darkness

One hundred and forty thousand kids are reported missing every year in the UK.[5,6] Of those some two-thirds are eventually recovered. What happens to the rest? That is the biggest secret and the answer could well take one to the highest echelons of our present-day culture. We shouldn't really blame the journalists, its too big an issue for them to grapple with. But the tide is turning, for sure.

Figure: Charles with Sir Jimmy Savile, OBE

Jimmy Savile was not only given Britain's top awards: knighted in 1990, Knight of Malta, Esteemed Friend of Israel, Order of the Garter, OBE in 1972 but also he was free to roam about Buckingham Palace. He could come and go whenever he wanted. Just as with the psychiatric hospitals and prisons where he preyed on the vulnerable, this serial paedophile also had licence to roam in the Prince of Wales's London base. After inveigling himself into Charles's life as a mentor and adviser, Savile was granted unprecedented access across all the royal palaces upstairs and downstairs.

Savile was a guest at Charles's 40th birthday party at Buckingham Palace in 1988, and then at his 50th. On Savile's 80th birthday, Charles sent him gold cufflinks and a message

---

[5] Hagiopian, 2000, p.113
[6] 'A Child is reported missing in the UK every three Minutes', *Mirror* 24.9.14 Abi Wilkinson

Nobody will ever know what you have done for this country Jimmy. This is to go some way in thanking you for that.

Readers may wish to ponder this. Savile told *Esquire* magazine, "The thing about me is I get things done and I work deep cover. I've known the Royal Family for a million years."[7] After his death (29.10.11), sanctimonious tributes were led by Prince Charles.

In 2014 *Time Magazine* carried a lead article on 'England, Land of the Royals, Tea and Horrific Pedophelia cover-ups.' (10.7.14) The public only started to learn about Savile's history of child sexual abuse in late 2012. What other commoner other than Jimmy Savile was allowed to roam at will around royal palaces? Who led the funeral tributes at Savile's funeral? Yes, it was Charles and Camilla. We should ask, how did British intel not advise against that action? So many now believe that the RF needs to be dismantled because of the pedo-connection.

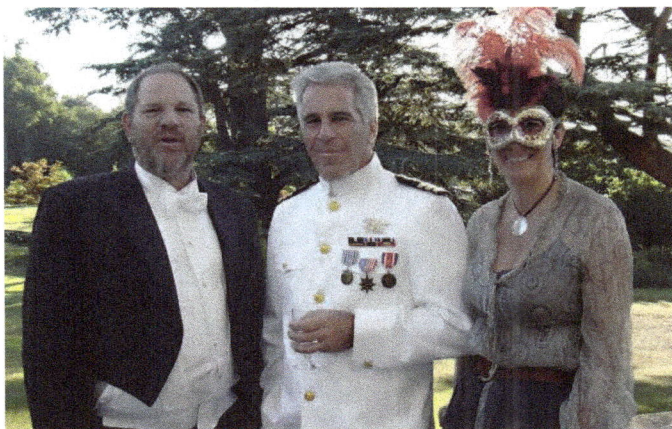

Figure: Ghislaine Maxwell, Harvey Weinstein and Jeffrey Epstein at Princess Beatrice's 18th birthday party in 2006 in the grounds of Windsor castle.

Ultimately, there is one and only one thing that royals are required to know about, and that is, *how to behave.* In any given situation they are required to conduct themselves *properly*, in a decent manner. Appearances

---

[7]   dailymail.co.uk/news/article-3122130/How-Savile-seduced-royals-s-claimed-nearly-godfather-Harry-predatory-DJ-wormed-way-heart-Palace-life.htmla

are what count. By way of illustration, consider the trio which Prince Andrew invited to the 18th birthday party of his daughter Beatrice.

One can hardly imagine a more sleazy trio, with Jeffrey Epstein mere months away from being arrested. The question is not so much 'How come Andrew was dumb enough to invite these child-molesting criminals to Windsor Castle?' But rather, how come no-one from the Palace or MI5 was checking the invites? Did Andrew not have anyone guiding him, to help avoid his personal, self-chosen path to catastrophe?

Joachim Hagopian has written a startling five volumes about *Satan, Sodomy and the Deep State,* which seem to be well-esteemed and carefully researched. His volume two concerns us, all 500-pages of it-

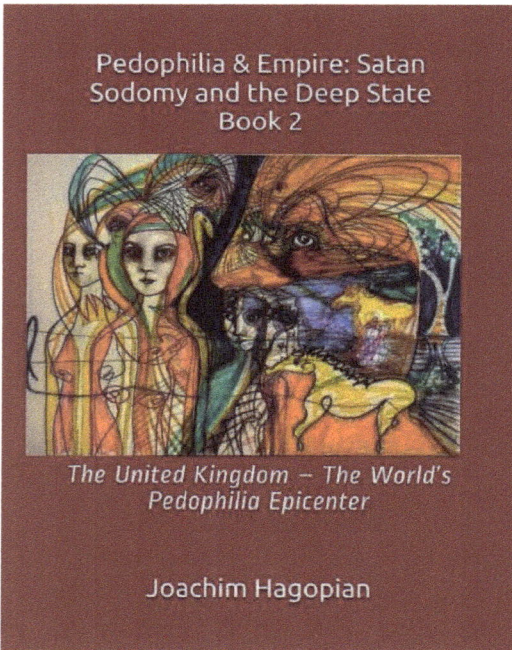

Pedophilia & Empire: Satan Sodomy and the Deep State Book 2

The United Kingdom – The World's Pedophilia Epicenter

Joachim Hagopian

Pedophilia and Empire: Satan, Sodomy and the Deep State, Book 2:

The United Kingdom – The World's Pedophilia Epicentre

Britain is, in his estimation, *paedo-capital of the world*. His book concerns the Matter of Britain, how it works, the glue that holds it together.[8] I have long felt we are living in a deeply evil culture in this 21st century, experiencing this through our country's dedication to Eternal War and the deceitful 'reasons for war' which this country will always brew up.[9] A different and complimentary angle emerges here.   Child sex slaves were being routinely pimped by

---

[8] pedoempire.org/contents/
[9] I've written a few books on this topic but they're not relevant here.

Savile. He's hailed as a 'national treasure' after his passing.[10] Savile assaults over a thousand kids in the BBC studios alone, girls aged ten to fifteen being his favourite, but young boys too. If they try to complain they're told to get lost. He would treat children's homes, care homes and girl's schools as 'boxes of chocolate' from which he could visit when he wished and select victims at will.

Police records totted up, came to 'Over 600 crimes of sexual abuse recorded against Savile in 28 police force areas across the UK' (p.133). He had total Palace protection, not least because he had gotten to know their secrets. The world's worst child-molesting rapist, necrophiliac and Satanist is allowed to go on a rampage over decades in the UK with his 'Jim'll Fix It' and pop music enterprises giving him unlimited access to young girls – and boys. When a policeman caught him in the act and tried to arrest him, he'd be told by his superior to back off, because Savile had top royal connections – he was protected.[11] Over decades it appears that the RF and specifically Charles was protecting this infernal sex-pest. 82% of his victims were reportedly female and 80% were children.[12]

He was Britain's most prolific child rapist of all time with at least 500 victims reportedly suffering at his hands. One account projects at least 1,000 victims sexually assaulted on *BBC* premises alone![13] These numbers include only registered abuse complaints to authorities on record, so the actual total of damaged souls can never be known but undoubtedly reaches into the thousands. He was raping both dead corpses and the most vulnerable, defenceless kids trapped inside British group homes and hospitals with the most creepy, unprecedented 24/7 access of any human being alive. One must alas agree with Hagopian that

> "A UK 'national treasure' has turned out to be both a satanic murdering corpse fucker and the biggest child rapist of all time."

---

[10] The extensive web-references given by Hagopian – over one thousand – are being scrubbed from the Web, often not even turning up in archive.org, the 'Wayback Machine.' 'Helpfreetheearth.com' seems to have been a good source, now gone.

[11] Hagopian, Ibid, p.101.

[12] 'Jimmy Savile Abuse: Number of Alleged Victims Reaches 450,' *BBC* (12.12.12). bbc.com/news/uk-20697738.

[13] D. Boffey, 'How Jimmy Savile Abused up to 1,000 victims of BBC Premises,' *The Guardian*, 18.1.14; Hagopian, p.104..

The Enveloping Darkness

The *BBC* elected to keep looking the other way for four straight decades. When police would sometimes question him, the arrogant Savile defiantly mocked his supposed interrogators knowing he was above the law, protected by his loyal, royal friends and prime minister allies who always had his back. He was able to select virtually any criminal insane asylum, mortuary, children's hospital, children's group home or school of his choice, along with the sprawling safe haven confines of his *BBC* conglomerate. Sir Jimmy Savile uniquely possessed at his personal disposal an unlimited supply of readymade victims. Dead corpses, debilitated children and adults alike as well as adoring underage fans, mostly girls but boys too - nobody was off limits to predator king Sir Jimmy.

Early accounts of him back in the 1980s have him as a necrophiliac, working in a morgue. Thus, the newly-dead received his semen. The Post Office had been using him on posters but they got rid of him upon learning of this practice. Many years later on Savile's 80th birthday Prince Charles gives him some gold cufflinks and a box of cigars with the affectionate words that we have cited above.

Savile supplied child victims to VIPs while working, in his own words, "deep cover" with British and foreign intelligence. How did he rise to the top? He did, to be sure, supply taxis full of to-be-molested kiddies for the pedo-parties, but also it seems that he was a safe pair of hands for disposing of the little kiddy corpses drained of blood once the satanic rituals were over: working in a morgue he thereby figured out a way to the top![14]

Of the brothers Andrew and Charles, Hagopian concluded: "The worst, most notorious pedophiles in the two most pedo-infested nations – the United Kingdom – Jimmy Savile, and in America – the Jeffrey Epstein -

---

[14] Refs: Daniel Boffey, "Revealed: How Jimmy Savile Abused up to 1,000 Victims on BBC Premises," *The Guardian*, January 18, 2014, theguardian.com/media/2014/jan/18/jimmy-savile-abused-1000-victims-bbc. Chris Greenwood and Martin Robinson, "Jimmy Savile got Rape Victim, 16, Pregnant and told her to Threaten Suicide if she was Denied an Abortion," *Daily Mail*, June 26, 2014, dailymail.co.uk/news/article-2670444/Jimmy-Savile-abused-corpses-boasted-jewellery-glass-eyes-NHS-report-reveals-shocking-new-details-paedophiles-crimes.html. telegraph.co.uk/news/uknews/crime/jimmy-savile/9795252/Jimmy-Savile-spent-every-waking-minute-thinking-about-abusing-boys-and-girls.html 11.1.13 express.co.uk/news/uk/370439/Jimmy-Savile-was-part-of-satanic-ring.

Gislaine Maxwell operation, were operatives working jointly for the CIA, MI6 and Mossad, the three biggest pedo-intel agencies in the world. And it's no wonder that Savile was King Charles' best buddy and Epstein was Prince Andrew's best buddy."[15]

Charles grew up close to Lord Louis Mountbatten, who was a member of the royal family, being the last great-grandchild of Queen Victoria. His official title was 'serene highness.' He was the Best Man at the wedding of Prince of Wales, he was mentor to the Queen, plus an honorary grandfather of Charles. His career was highly successful, as he became Viceroy of India, a top NATO commander, the First Sea Lord and then Chief of the Defence Staff in the UK.

His Serene Highness Lord Mountbatten was a prolific pedophile and sodomite. Andrew Lownie, the respected modern biographer, has described this long-denied aspect of Mountbatten's life. Rent-boys would be delivered to NATO HQ for *use by Mountbatten*. His preference was for little Indian boys but also, he did like 'beautiful boys in school uniform.'[16] Those abused children are likely to have a life irrevocably damaged, as the sparkle of innocence and hope is extinguished and also children thus abused have a tendency to, later on, do the same to others by way of coping with the trauma.[17] When Mountbatten was staying in Malta, his chauffeur was instructed to checkout the local male brothel for him. As Lownie remarked to Gemma O'Doherty, "It's not a way to get on in life by suggesting that members of the Royal Family were pedophiles."[18]

It could be a sign of hope that a modern historian can reveal such things and yet retain his status, as Fellow of the Royal Historical Society, etc. His best-selling book revealed how any crime of Prince Andrew was quite insignificant compared to those of Mountbatten. The royals are left with

> 'The legacy of Lord Mountbatten, a gigantic figure in the Windsor dynasty, and the centre of the most troubling allegations of sexual crimes against children.'[19]

---

[15] Hagopian on sott.net, 22.4.24: 'Tucker Carlson finally blows the pedophilia lid off on puppet control.'
[16] Andrew Lownie, *The Mountbattens*, 2019, p.357.
[17] For Mountbatten himself abused as a child, see Lownie, Ibid., p.366.
[18] robertdavidsteele.com/the-lurid-world-of-pedophile-lord-louis-mountbatten/
[19] Frankreport.com 'Lord Mountbatten: the Grandfather of all British Royal Sex Scandals'

Mountbatten liked working in the Royal Navy, because of its ethic of obedience and not telling stories. Good-looking young officers would be invited to his office, where they'd be startled to discover that they would have to bend over, etc, as a key to promotion. But, there was one occasion when, placing his hand upon the knee of the ship's medical officer and propositioning him, he found himself rebuffed:

'What about your career?' asked Mountbatten.

'You don't understand,' replied the Doctor. 'I'm planning to make a career outside the Navy.'

(Lownie, page 357) Because the doctor was looking forward to a future career outside the royal navy, therefore he could decline the offer, of receiving the royal semen.

Lownie tells how Mountbatten was in a relation with the serial killer Roy Fontaine, author of *To Kill and Kill again: the Chilling true confessions of a Serial Killer* (2002) — which does seem most appropriate for a NATO Supreme Commander. Fontaine's biographer Mr Pender asked him, 'You mean - you mounted Mountbatten?'

'No', Roy replied, ever a stickler for detail, 'Mountbatten mounted me. He believed it is better to give than to receive.'

Pender asked Fontaine what he called his royal lover, to which the response was: 'Most of Mountbatten's gay friends called him "Mountbottom"'

'Did you call him Mountbottom?'

'Of course not. That could have been disrespectful ... I called him the Queen'[20]

Years later, Princess Diana disliked what she called the 'pink mafia' of the Palace that was surrounding her kids. Commented her biographer Neil Botham,

---

[20] Lownie Ibid, p.354.

Lord Mountbatten, known affectionately as the biggest queen in the royal family, had surrounded Charles with homosexuals during the period when he had been entrusted by Queen Elizabeth with her eldest son's social upbringing. Diana did not like the clique that was similarly intended to be around her two sons and had systematically got rid of over 40 gay members of her husband's staff by forcing resignations or personally firing them.'[21]

Anthony Blunt the Queen's art curator (and distant relative 3rd cousin) was stoutly defended by her when found guilty of treason. In 1979 he was exposed for betraying spy secrets to the Soviet Union, revealed by PM Margaret thatcher in the House of commons, and stripped on his knighthood. As a pedophile he was too high up ever to be prosecuted. He had a macabre penchant for 'asphyxiating child victims, causing their bodies to contract to heighten the orgasm for the sodomiser' (Hagopian p.291).

The Right Reverend Peter Ball is the most senior member of the Church of England to have been arrested for offenses against children. He was arrested on eight suspected cases of abuse against boys and young men ranging from ages 12 to 20 during the 1980s to 1990s. As the former Bishop of Gloucester he resigned in 1993 after being served with a police caution for "committing an act of gross indecency against a teenager." Upon his resignation, Ball retired to Manor Lodge, 'a wisteria-clad property owned by the Duchy of Cornwall.' In reference to his new living arrangements, Ball stated, "He (Prince Charles) has been wonderfully kind and allowed me to have a duchy house. The prince is a loyal friend. I have immense admiration for him, he has been through horrific times and is a great person."

Pertinently comment Brandon Turberville: "At the very least, the Prince is the absolute worst judge of character who ever lived." [22]

If his judgement is really that bad, is he fit to be king?

---

[21] Noel Botham, *The Murder of Princess Diana*, 2004, p.53; Hagopian, p.52.
[22] activistpost.com/2012/11/the-prince-and-pedophile-charles.html 16.11.12

3

Lady Di and the Paternity of Her Children

Who can forget the wonderful royal wedding back in 1981, a day that captivated hearts around the globe? I happened to know the lady who became Lady Diana Spencer's astrologer (Penny Thornton), and she assured me that Diana swore to her that Charles had slept with Camilla on the night before the wedding. Charles was unfaithful to Diana right from the get-go. He lied outrageously in front of the altar, in Saint Paul's Cathedral, before the Archbishop of Canterbury, deceiving all the British people with his wedding vows which he had not the slightest intention of honouring. In the words of one biographer, this 'tragic young woman was cuckolded even before she approached the altar' and Charles 'courted Diana with deliberate lies.'[23]

Just prior to the wedding Diana came across some 'wedding presents' that Charles was giving out to friends. One was to Camilla: a gold ring with the initials 'GF' engraved upon them. We may all guess what 'GF' stands for and it probably wasn't (with reference to the tampon remark) 'Girl Friday,' as Charles explained to Diana when she asked. Di enquired about backing out from the wedding as the full horror-scope of the situation dawned upon her, but was told by her pals 'Bad luck Duch, your face is on the tea-towels' ('Duch' being their term of endearment for her, the 'Duchess'). She felt, she said, like a lamb going to the slaughter.

Wonderful strains of the Holst Jupiter music sounded through St Paul's cathedral as the royal couple walked down the aisle. But hang on, let's hear the words -

> *"I vow to thee, my country..*
> *The love that asks no questions,*
> *That lays upon the altar the*
> *dearest and the best..*
> *The love that makes undaunted*

---

[23] Noel Botham, *The Murder of Princess Diana,* 2007, pp.xxiv, xxix.

the final sacrifice."

Yes, she did that. For us.

On the honeymoon aboard the royal yacht while having dinner Diana noticed the cufflinks which Charles was wearing, being engraved with 'C&C'. They were a present, Charles explained, from Camilla. It was indeed as Diana said in her *Panorama* interview 'a crowded marriage;' as in 'What the hell is that woman doing here?' Camilla became the regular, every-night feature of Diana's nightmares. She would allude to her as 'Camilla park-your-balls' (Parker-Bowles) and as 'the Rottweiler.' How frightening it must have been seeing Camilla's face close-up, it's bad enough for us having to see it in photographs.

Charles treated Lady Di as little more than a hired womb, who produced 'the heir and the spare,' in her words. After that she could be disposed of. Her time spent as *Her Royal Highness*, which inspired the entire Planet Earth with a Queen-of-Hearts image of Our Princess - the only one in my lifetime - she came to remember as 'twelve fucking diabolical years.'[24]

Figure: A happy family trio

Mannakee

The case of Barry Mannakee displays the level of cruelty and enjoyment of casual death, displayed by Charles towards his wife. Police Sergeant

---

[24] Botham, p.73.

Lady Di and the Paternity of Her Children

Mannakee became Di's official minder in 1985, and soon acquired the role of guarding Prince William. He and the Princess were close and some reckoned they were too close - even though, as Botham assures us, he as a bodyguard did not do the forbidden thing: he was, after all, married with two children (Botham p.26). Di was not a home-wrecker. He was a good shoulder to cry on and he would listen to her stories. There came a time when it was reckoned, in certain quarters, that he 'knew too much,' maybe about Charles' liason with Camilla. Therefore, he had to go, he was relieved of royal duties. But that, it turned out, was not enough, he also had to die in a motorcycle 'accident'. As a former senior intelligence officer expressed, his death could have been arranged:

> 'This type of fatal accident is not difficult to set up. Clearly other people would have to be involved but witnesses, if there were any, would not necessarily remember seeing them.' (Botham, p.29)

Diana always remained sure that Manakee's death had been arranged. Thus, James Hewitt had for years been Diana's lover and was the father of Harry. Hewitt recalled how Nicholas Soames, the Tory MP and grandson of Churchill, warned him to back off from his liason with Diana, or else 'I could meet the same fate as Barry Mannakee.' (Botham p.29) That surely leaves us in no doubt, that Diana was correct in her view on her bodyguard's sudden death.

Diana was notified of Mannakee's death by Charles. As the couple were on their way to the Cannes Film Festival and were getting out of a car, he said to her:

> 'O by the way, I got news from the protection unit yesterday that poor Barry Mannakee was killed. Some sort of motorcycle accident. Terrible shame, isn't it?'

As Di burst into tears, Charles pushed her out of the car saying: 'Let's go darling, your press awaits you!' He was here enjoying the way he could get the person killed who was then closest to Di, for no especial reason. She was being kept in a gilded cage, not allowed to get close to anyone. The death would have been on his orders. No wonder she came to fear for her own life. Di would make a yearly pilgrimage to the crematorium where the ashes of Mannakee were scattered.

Lady Di and the Paternity of Her Children

Months before her death Diana wrote a letter to her butler Paul Burrell saying ""*This particular phase of my life is the most dangerous - My husband is planning 'an accident' in my car, brake failure and serious head injury.*" Quite a few others have recalled Diana having made some such statement to them (Hagopian, p.90). The police hung onto the Burrell letter for six years before releasing it.

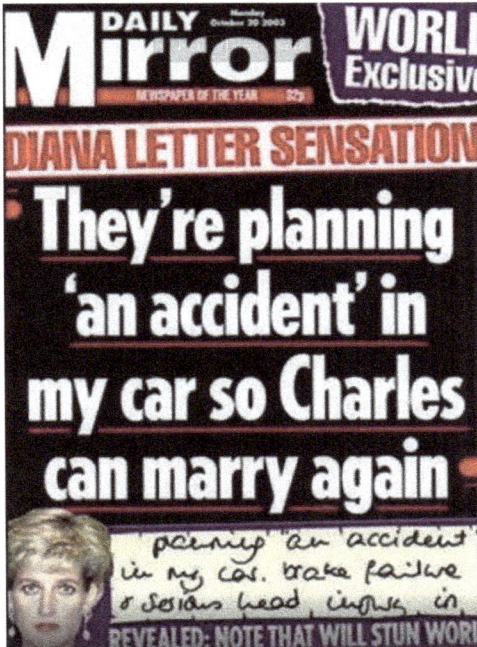

Figure: *Daily Mirror* front page, 20.10.03

Lady Di was highly intuitive and probably a bit psychic, for that is *precisely* what happened to her. It was the *moira* of her fate. Had she not brilliantly fulfilled her life at six and thirty years? As our Queen of Hearts was there anything else she could have done? She was about to announce that she was expecting a child from her new fiancé Dodi Fayed, and The Powers That Be would not have been able to endure a Muslim child. It would be unthinkable. Why, world peace might have broken out! Also, she had charmed Bill Clinton into supporting a ban on landmines which the US Military-Industrial-Complex could hardly tolerate. He reneged on that commitment right after her death. Also, the British royals were fed up with being perpetually in the shadows, as grumpy old gits who could never compete with Di. Thus, the Axis of Evil, viz. the US-UK military intelligence, decided to get rid of her.

For uninformed readers who accept the established narrative - that her death was an accident caused by a drunk driver and Di failing to buckle up her seat belt – see Appendix, but for now and without undue detail, the driver Henri Paul had had only a minimal drop of alcohol beforehand and by no stretch of the imagination could he be described as drunk; nor was he speeding, travelling at 65 km/hr on a main arterial route through Paris.

Lady Di and the Paternity of Her Children

In the tunnel there was a motorcyclist ahead of them who turned around and let off a brilliant flashlight to dazzle the driver, causing him to hit the 13th column: under the *Pons d'Alma,* the 'Bridge of Souls.' She died, not in the tunnel, but in the ambulance, which took an extremely long time, well over one hour, to reach the hospital. All of the CCTV cameras along and around the Alma tunnel, which was their chosen route, were not working, their film all turned out to be unavailable - an *unfailing indicator* of state collusion: it was a high-level event.[25]

A jury scrutinising the circumstances of her death reached a conclusion of 'unlawful killing,' a polite circumlocution for murder, in April of 2008. (Watch the film 'unlawful killing' at sott.net). Charles could then get on with marrying Camilla, exactly as Diana had foreseen.

There is only one thing in my lifetime that would have made the people of England deliriously happy, and that is, Di becoming our Queen. All Charles would have had to do to become king would have been to refrain from expressing his funny opinions and hang onto his glorious princess. But Oh no, he couldn't do that. It was her beauty itself which he didn't like; which repelled him... He just had to desire an ugly, married, older woman and in 1994 he confessed to adultery on prime-time TV with Richard Dimbleby.

Then, there was his tampax remark. To give credit to the British press they did manage to remain silent over this remark – how Prince Charles had drooled over the phone that he wished he could remain stuffed between Camilla's legs as a tampax roll – mum was the word, for months, until eventually it was released Down Under. After that it was all over the tabloids. Anyone with a vestige of moral sense would have appreciated, that that should have precluded him from inheriting the Crown of England – as 'defender of the Faith', head of the Church of England.

William was conceived mere months after the royal wedding, and one may surmise that initially Di was faithful to Charles, hoping against hope that she could get the marriage to work. She threw herself down the stairs when four months pregnant, as if in despair over Charles' infidelity. If indeed it was Charles' child then that could account for why she would do

---

[25] For comparison, at the Pentagon on 9/11, there were 83 cameras that could have caught the impact, but were 'not working.'

so terrible a thing. Evidently, little William was tough and determined to emerge.

Hewitt

Three years after the wedding things were (I suggest) different. By then her companion was James Hewitt, who helped rescue her sanity.

Both Harry's bio and another by James Hewitt stated categorically that the affair only started a year or two after Harry was born. But, a West-End play had adopted a different view. Composed in 2015 as a result of its author enjoying extensive conversations with Mr Hewitt, it played for a week in the West End.

Truth, Lies, Diana in their own Words was billed as 'a remarkable new British play straight from New York.' Of his ground-breaking, 'factional' drama, author John Conway explained, 'I have been talking to James over a period of two years. I met him and he told me some quite remarkable things that have never been said in the public domain, particularly about when his relationship with Diana started.' Journalists consulted James Hewitt who endorsed the play:

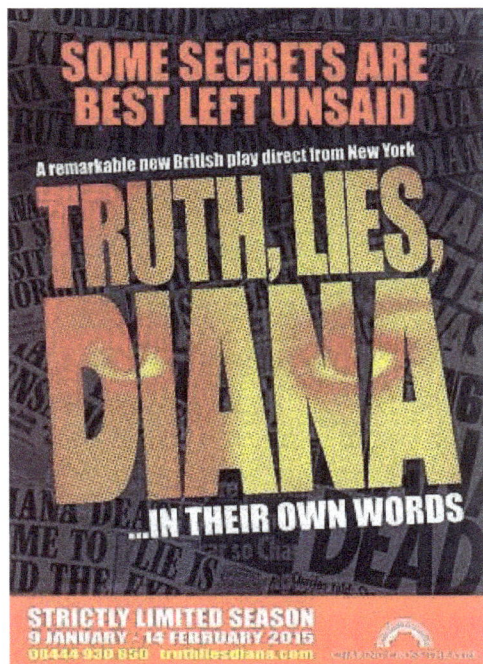

Hewitt, 56, last night confirmed that he knows author John Conway and spoke to him about his relationship with Diana, and said he had no doubt the play would be 'accurate'.

Figure: the West-End play by John Conway

The play alleges that Household Cavalry officer James Hewitt started his affair with Princess Diana of Wales prior to the conception of her second son, Prince Harry, in 1984. Based on interviews, official statements and court transcripts from those closest to the late princess, including Hewitt, it also hints that her former lover might be the young prince's biological father, as many have speculated for years.[26]

Figure: Diana takes Harry to see James Hewitt at an army camp

"Diana and I started our relationship more than a year before Harry was born," Hewitt's character says in the play. "Now that doesn't prove that I am his father. It's just the ... inconvenient truth." "There is a startling revelation that James Hewitt makes, and he has allowed me to make it in the play," Conway said. "That is the fact that his relationship with Diana started 18 months before Prince Harry was born. We are not saying that he is Prince Harry's father, although the audience may take their own view on that."

The *Daily Mail's* review stated: 'Outrage over James Hewitt's backing for West End Play about Princess Diana that suggests he may be Prince Harry's

---

[26] The two would meet up in Marbella, Spain: 'Europe's Rich & Famous: the Luxurious Life of Marbella Spain' (36 min) by Piers Morgan has Harry and Hewitt staying there, being adjacent to each other in the video, though tactfully avoiding saying they met.

father. The Author claims Hewitt told him 'remarkable things' and that he sent him 15 pages of the script for approval'.[27]

The play brings John Morgan onto the stage as the investigator. He's the author of *Paris-London connection, the Assassination of Princess Diana* (2012) a frighteningly detailed book which tells you more than you need to know about the carefully-planned event.

Here is a picture of a happy Diana with the young Prince Harry and James Hewitt in 1989. It says quite a lot.

In the bedroom of James Hewitt at his country home in Wiltshire, there is just one picture hanging on his wall. It is of the young Prince Harry. Noel Botham, author of *The Murder of Princess Diana*, questioned him about it and 'he declined, very politely, to give an explanation.' (p.48) Mr Hewitt has to deny and keep silent about the best experience of his life.[28]

I co-manage a deep politics or, 'conspiracy discussion' group which has met monthly over the years, and it went *en masse* to see the play, then its author was invited to give a talk to our group. His play didn't explicitly state that Hewitt fathered Prince Harry – no production taking such a view could have performed in the West End - but it went as far as it could, revealing when the two linked up prior to Harry's conception. *Harry was Hewitt's child*, though the various parties are obliged to deny it. Harry's self-identity depends upon his being Prince Harry: is he not the son of the King?

---

[27]   dailymail.co.uk/news/article-2888733/New-Diana-play-based-real-interviews-features-James-Hewitt-saying-started-relationship-year-Harry-born-doesn-t-prove-m-father-s-just-inconvenient-truth.html
youtube.com/watch?v=CPknQ1KZ1S4 *Truth, Lies Diana* at the Charing cross Theatre; also youtube.com/watch?v=Pc1J55_AKbg

[28] As earlier proposed by Ian Halperin in 2009 (NY Times bestselling author and winner of the *Rolling Stone Magazine* Award for Investigative *Journalism):* "A longtime employee of Harry's mother Princess Diana told IUC that the Royal Family was involved in a massive coverup to hide the fact that Diana's ex-lover James Hewitt is Harry's real father. According to the source Prince Philip threatened Hewitt's life if he didn't go along with the coverup. "They made him lie about the timeline," the source told IUC. "Prince Philip told Hewitt he would destroy him if it ever leaked out. It's impossible that Charles is Harry's real father. Hewitt was on the scene as Diana's lover two years before Harry was born. Diana stopped having sex with Charles years before Harry was born. Harry looks exactly like Hewitt." (`IUC World Exclusive: Prince Charles Not Harry's Real Father; Ex-Diana Lover Keeps Silent Because of Death Threats From Royal Family', *find it using archive.org. IUC =IanUnderCover)*

Lady Di and the Paternity of Her Children

Erm, no. He is always going to be a damaged, tormented character, easy for Meghan to manipulate. He lacks the intelligence to comprehend the identity of his mother's assassins, and will at the drop of a hat blame the paparazzi who pursued her, as if they had somehow caused the crash. Well he knows who his father is but is never allowed to mention it, presumably not even to Meghan, otherwise she would have undue power over him. The Palace can strip him of all his royal honours and proud army titles - and it has not yet done so – and terminate his Palace funding, but can't remove the 'Prince' title he was born with.

Figure: Harry and his father James Hewitt

Figure: A young Harry with his father on the right

Younger pictures of the two are more comparable, where both share the same flaming red hair.

Teetering on the brink of extinction and with ever-declining public support, Britain's royal family cannot permit the truth to emerge. British taxpayers coughed up thirty million for Harry's wedding to a Californian divorcee actress, who turned out to have little or no interest in serving as a member of the RF. She wanted the glamor and the glitz, the snazzy titles – Duchess of Sussex etc … The huge damage those two have caused to the RF can (I suggest) be understood in terms of Harry's estrangement, his not being the son of Charles.

The old Queen passed away having seen both her son Andrew and her grandson Harry deleted from the RF, whereby everything, the very future of the monarchy, comes to depend upon Prince William. Can he shoulder so great a burden? Does he want to? How is it possible that a millennium-old monarchy has come to depend upon one person? For sure we'd all like to see a DNA check of the British royals but that is unlikely ever to happen.

4

Charles III, Owner of one-sixth of the Earth

The 25th anniversary of Lady Di's death takes us from the tragedy of August 1997 to August 31, 2022. Then merely days later on 8th of September 2022 Britain's longest-ruling queen – ever, in history - passes away. Her elder son Charles assumes the mantle of kingship. The old Queen had managed to hold everything together, just about, despite the goings on of her royal offspring. She was wise enough not to shoot her mouth off about all sorts of topics while managing to give the impression that she did really care about our well-being, that of her own subjects. The length of her reign, seventy years, contributed so much to the stability of the realm. She gave form to our very sense of being British.

Whereas, who now wants to see Charles' head on the currency? Things start to fall to pieces after the passing of our Queen. *Two years* after her death, the currency still has her head on it. One meets people who have seen Charles' head on the currency, but – it's rare! Or, do the authorities belive he will die soon, and are therefore not keen to change the currency to have his head on it?

'Operation Menai Bridge' is the code for the preparations for Charles' death – all royals have 'bridge' codewords for their ceremony of departure – and is now well underway.

Figure: Crown with the Koh-i-Noor diamond, stolen from India in 1849.

Charles has purchased not one but two ancient properties around Transylvania. He explained that 'Transylvania is in my blood. The genealogy shows that I am descended from Vlad the Impaler, so I do have a bit of a stake in the country.' After his wife Lady Di had been bumped off, and Kate – another Princess of Wales – seemed to have vanished mysteriously, one might expect him to have been more circumspect with such remarks. In 2017 he was officially honoured with the title "Prince of Transylvania."[29]

The Romanian government is promoting tourism on the basis of the British royals having ancestral links to brutal Vlad the Impaler. Let's hope this story doesn't get any worse.

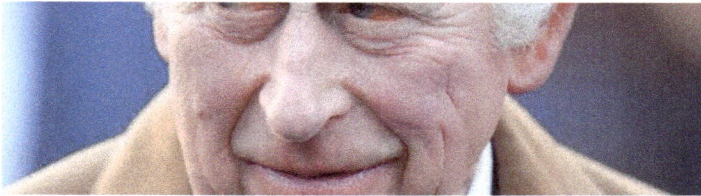

Figure: Charles: Descended from Vlad the Impaler?

Once crowned king, Charles set about proselytising about a ten-point plan for the World Economic Forum.[30] Together with his buddy Klaus Schwaab he helped to push the monster Covid hoax, where the new 'vaccines' have caused so much long-term damage to the human race. The World Economic Forum agenda involves the dissolving of national boundaries for its one-world agenda, and as such, for a British monarch, that could be considered treason.

People wondered who or what Charles could be alluding to in one of his WEF speeches:

'Here we need a vast military-style campaign to marshal the strength of the global private sector. With trillions at its disposal, far beyond global GDP, and with the greatest respect beyond even the governments of the world's leaders.'

Listen to it on Youtube. Was he channelling the anti-Christ, people wondered? Who else has 'trillions at his disposal,' riches 'far beyond global GDP', beyond the reach of 'even the governments of the world's

---

[29] C Tominey, 'Prince of Transylvania: Charles honoured as the kin of Vlad the Impaler', *Express* 16.4.17

[30] D Uria, 'Prince Charles Introduces ten-point Climate plan at WEF' UPI, 22.1.20

leaders'? Whatever delusional condition is afflicting him here, he had no business as King of England to go prattling on about it. It sounds highly treasonous, whatever it is. And, by the way, your royal highness, carbon dioxide is good for Planet Earth.

Figure: The red-coloured 'infernal' view of the royal portrait, composed by Rick Savage. Savile is pointing to a monarch butterfly on Charles' right shoulder. As regards the original - the first official portrait since Charles became King - here is a comment by جرائم المسلم النازي: 'This picture answers many questions. The son follows in his father's footsteps, and it seems that there is no salvation for man from the evil of these people. O Creator, be kind to us.'

For anyone who thinks that British imperialism is a thing of the past, Charles as the new King has inherited *one-sixth of the Earth,* which tots up to six billion acres. Thus, any Australian wishing to buy a house can only in fact purchase a lease on land already owned by the Windsor family. The English monarch has a prior claim on the property! It's far from easy to understand why Australians should find such an arrangement acceptable.

5

The Doom of Prince Andrew

O, The grand old Duke of York

He had twelve million quid

He gave it to an American girl

For something he 'never did.'

In 2000 Prince Andrew brought Jeffrey Epstein and Ghislaine Maxwell to the Queen's birthday as his personal guests. No-one has ever figured out what exactly Epstein did or where his wealth came from, but the two of them seem to have been Mossad agents. Around that time one gains the impression that Andrew was being manipulated and entrapped by sexual blackmail using minors, without quite realising what was happening. Or ... were those two just his best friends?

> 'It is a matter of record that Epstein was seeking out rich and powerful individuals and entrapping them with minors for the purpose of blackmail. The fact that personal friends of Epstein and Maxwell at the time openly stated that their "manipulative" relationship with Prince Andrew was "very premeditated" and "probably being done for Epstein" strongly suggests that not only was the Prince entrapped, but that this type of entrapment activity was known to occur among those who were close to Epstein and Maxwell at the time.'[31]

One would appreciate Andrew's story about who exactly Jeffrey Epstein was, he could surely tell us quite a bit about Epstein's mysterious rise to fame from being just an obscure school math teacher to one who seemed to know all the rich and famous. But there was a limit to how much could be covered up: 'Andrew attended naked pool parties and was treated to massages by a harem of adolescent girls.'[32] Sounds like heaven, but he

---

[31]   mintpressnews.com/scrubbed-reports-reveal-new-secrets-of-the-prince-andrew-jeffrey-epstein-relationship/262330/

[32] Hagopian p.62, quoting *Vanity Fair* 29.6.11 Prince Andrew: Ties to Geoffrey Epstein'

went too far, not comprehending the entrapment being woven, as if no-one had drummed into him the necessary conditions for the RF's survival. Andrew's closest associates kept getting busted as 'VIP pedophiles and pedo-pimp trafficers.' (Hagopian, p.64) Andrew's ex-wife Sarah Ferguson was a long-time close friend of Ghislaine Maxwell and may have introduced him.

Andrew finally paid out twelve million pounds to Virginia Guiffre in February of 2022 after denying he had met her. The Queen helped him out here, it was mainly her money. Most of us (or, most men I should add) can't see a lot wrong in having a fling with a beautiful, seventeen year old girl, still less how a man is supposed to defend himself against alleged rape of twenty years ago, when there is no evidence of duress. (Andrew met Guiffre in 2001, she brought her case against him in 2022). It is his attempt to deny that liason for which he will be most remembered.

He had long been close with Jeffrey Epstein, whose diary was found to have a variety of his phone numbers, both private and at the Palace, more than anyone else, and in addition he went on a load of holidays with Ghislaine Maxwell. Andrew finally doomed himself with the 'incoherent train-wreck of an interview' he gave to the BBC in November 2019 and turned himself into a joke with his Pizza-Express-at-Woking alibi about THAT photograph. That marked his exit from royal life. He remains a Knight of the Garter but no longer is he the Duke of York. Stripped of his job as Britain's trade envoy in 2011 he's still worth a cool fifty million, not least due to his having siphoned off taxpayer's money into various Caribbean tax-haven accounts.

Had the court case of Ms Guiffre gone ahead, Meghan Markle was due to be called as a witness, when rumours of her as a 'yacht girl' with Andrew might have emerged. The Palace paid a lot to stop that disclosure. Meghan's brother-in-law Thomas Markle Junior avers that she used to be a yacht girl, citing a video reviewing the yacht-girl culture which mentions her name several times.[33] Did a royal wedding really take place with a woman who hired out her body in this way? Prior to the wedding, British intel worked hard deleting MM stories and porn-images from the Web.

---

[33] youtube.com/watch?v=xYpyol-AzUE Yacht girl culture

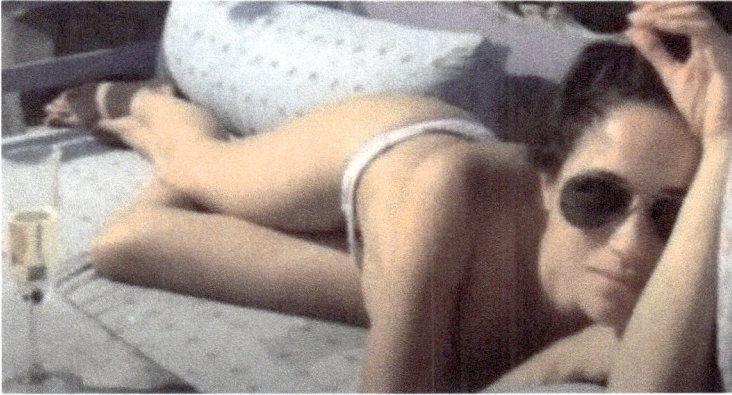

Figure: Meghan as Yacht-girl: connections to Epstein and Prince Andrew?[34]

In 2006, Epstein, together with alleged pimp Ghislaine Maxwell and disgraced film mogul Harvey Weinstein were at the 18th birthday party of Andrew's daughter Beatrice. The police had already prepared an arrest warrant for Epstein on child sex-abuse charges and eight days after this event he was in cuffs. Commented a Palace aide: 'This photograph sums up just why the Epstein affair has been so disastrous for Andrew. He brought these people into the royal fold, to Windsor Castle no less, where they could rub shoulders with the great and the good. It is an astounding lack of judgement at the very least.'

Almost as bad, indeed, as the Queen giving the Order of the Garter knighthood to Tony Blair, or Charles leading the tributes at the funeral service of Jimmy Savile.

State papers on Andrew remain closed until 2065, plus official computers have been wiped for anything to do with him and persons who had dealings with him had to sign NDAs – as a trade envoy was he really that bad? Formerly second-in-line to the throne he's now a nobody. The sixty-odd teddy bears in his bedroom still have to be lined up in a row, his staff would receive training as to how to do this. He'll now have plenty of time to talk to them.

---

[34] Youtube, 'Royal Massive': *Proof that Meghan was a Yacht Girl A Toronto Native confirms Harry's wife a Yacht Girl for Andrew* 2023

6

The Children of Kate

Kate and William got married in April 2011. A year and a half went by with no pregnancy, then finally, in late December 2012, did she become pregnant? Consider these three dates:

2-6 December 2012 Kate in hospital: her pregnancy was announced.

15 June 2013 She attends the Trooping of the Colour, while she was surely not pregnant (see image).

22 July The birth of 'George' by Kate is reported.

Figure: Kate at Trooping of Colour ceremony, supposedly eight months pregnant

She has thin, boyish hips: fashion mags marvel at how she kept her 'incredible' 24" waist after having three children. Seen from behind one might guess she was a boy. Was she told she could never give birth, that it could be fatal, or maybe she did not want a cesarean?

Kate was admitted to hospital on December 2, allegedly with 'morning sickness,' a condition which can afflict pregnant women. The public were

The Children of Kate

given to understand that she was 4-8 weeks pregnant. Medical staff at the royal estate could well have treated that condition, which hardly needs a hospital visit. More likely, she was brought to the hospital for *egg removal surgery*: 'in vitro' fertilization takes a few days, so after an HCG injection, egg retrieval from Kate's ovaries would have taken between 34 and 36 hours. [HGC is a 'trigger shot' which indicates the final maturation of the ovum. Used with timed intercourse it increases the chances of pregnancy] Embryo transfer into the surrogate woman's uterus would have been done three days after fertilization, so the birth would have been due around September 5th, 2013 – a full two months *after* the date announced.

<u>Figure:</u> Kate with slim hips

After the pregnancy of George was announced, in December, Kate's nurse at the hospital, Jacintha Saldanha, 'committed suicide' by hanging herself with her scarf. Here is a US news report:

It was first reported this week that Kate Middleton was pregnant with her first child with Prince William. But the celebration came to an abrupt halt Friday after a nurse from the hospital where Kate was admitted for severe morning sickness, was found dead. Her name was Jacintha Saldanha a 47-year old mother of two. (ENTV)

She was found dead on 7 December, 2012, the day after Kate went home. Was her nurse about to spill the beans? A cover story was quickly brewed up, that she had been upset by a couple of prank phone calls from Australia. Does that sound likely? Would you commit suicide after a prank phone call? She had been working for a few years at the hospital, showing no sign of being unstable, nor was she being reprimanded or disciplined. However she did have access to Kate's medical records, i.e. *she knew too much.* Her body was found to have injury marks on its wrist, suggesting a final struggle with her killer(s).

People were shocked at how thin Kate became, weighing only 95 pounds while pregnant. Was she too thin to bear an heir, in fact thinner than she had been six years previously? Was her frail frame not borderline anorexic? Her obsession with a twiggy fashion-queen body-image may have caused her weight to plunge to 92 pounds at the time of her pregnancy. Pregnant women are advised by doctors never to wear high heels in the third trimester due to problems of balance, of her back and swelling issues, so how come she wore them? People noticed that her bump would seem to come and go and slip about.

Many commented on how it hardly looked as if she'd been pregnant. Photos of her posing in high heels wearing make-up and holding the baby on the hospital steps raised more suspicion. Was it a doll? 'It's the first time we've seen him' commented William, as the royal couple stood on the steps of the maternity hospital holding 'George' - which didn't sound right. Here is the full quote, to help you decide:

> "He's a big boy, he's quite heavy. We are still working on a name so we will have that as soon as we can. It's the first time we have seen him really so we are having a proper chance to catch up."

Was William being a bit too candid here?

Holding the baby, Kate appeared wearing the very 'Rosemary's baby' red dress that Mia Farrow had worn in the film, when giving birth to the devil. Surely that has to have been *intended* to stir up gossip? It certainly did that!

Kate had not shown typical signs of water retention during advanced pregnancy such as facial fullness, puffiness or breast, ankle and feet swelling and in fact she looked just as slender and comfortable in heels as she had before her alleged pregnancy. Her stomach didn't grow large enough to have carried a baby of eight pounds, six ounces, George's official birth weight. It appeared as brown-eyed, a dominant eye colour that no one on William's side for two generations had carried.

Here are some of the sceptical comments –

- 'If she really gave birth naturally, it was surely some days ago.'
- 'Look at the baby – he does not look like a newborn at all. He is at least three days old.
- 'There is nothing which would help a woman, even if she gave birth with the help of best doctors, stand up five hours after giving birth – and leave the clinic on her feet.'
- 'It was a surrogate mother who gave birth but not her.'
- "Would be so amazing to have narrow hips, a flat tummy and no stretch marks so soon after giving birth."
- 'Kate must have been wearing a fake belly... It is just not real to walk yourself several hours after birth and wave to the public.'
- It was 'impossible for Kate to look so radiant'.
- 'She did not give birth, I am sure,' said one. 'There is no special maternal look in her eyes – this natural thing is not visible. Look at Diana. This Kate is just an actress from Buckingham Palace theatre. She never gave birth!'
- The way she hardly looks or touches the baby while on the stairs of St Mary's proves it.
- 'Only men and girls who never gave birth can believe in this story.'
- I've said for some time that it often appears as if she's been wearing a pregnancy suit (fake boobs and bump). Today we were proved right.

After 'George' was born a deep silence ensued. No office had witnessed the birth, though that is the royal custom. What one may call the real George seems only to have appeared a month or two *after* the media-hyped 'birth.' The mean duration of gestation is 263 days or nine lunar months. The reported birth date was eight months after her hospital visit. These things would account for the furtive manner in which Kate was hustled off to her parental residence after the alleged birth: there was *no baby of hers* for her to show off.

She had decided not to hire a maternity nurse. What, no maternity nurse? A source told the *Daily Mail* that "Kate just feels safest and most secure when she's with her family." Wasn't William supposed to be her family? How come she was moving back in with her parents? Why isn't William around to participate as a parent?[35]

Figure: Three happy children, from an unknown mother, their DNA from Kate and William.

The baby could not be an heir because it had not been born from the body of the wife of the legal heir to the throne. Some even conjectured, that it may not have been from William's seed. They saw an odd distancing of the RF from George and the Middletons and noted the very strange Christening with many of the senior Royals missing.[36]

In fact, during all three of her pregnancies, it seemed as though her bump was fake, as if she'd been wearing a silicone pregnancy belly, enabling her rapid return to a sylph-like figure. Had she not hired a

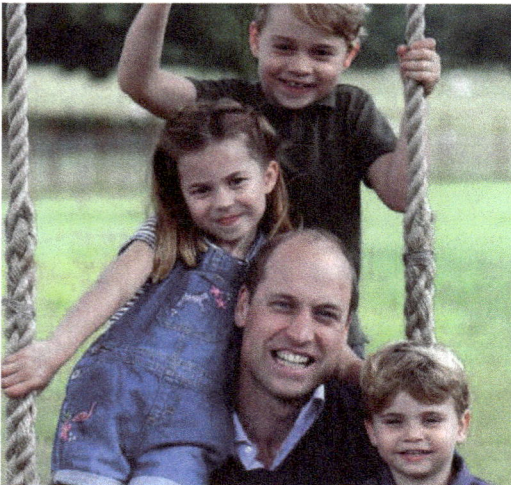

"surrogate" to avoid the morning sickness, weight gain, swollen ankles and breasts, bladder discomfort, labour, pain and stretch marks of pregnancy to escape the havoc that pregnancy would wreak on her shapely, underweight body and her fashionable royal lifestyle?

---

[35]   https://thecolemanexperience.wordpress.com/2014/09/11/is-kate-middleton-really-pregnant/ Insert into 'archive.org', for Kate never having been pregnant.
[36] helpfreetheearth.com/news825_kate.html   (deleted)

The Children of Kate

A couple of bent doctors were required. Dr. F. became engaged to Jill Dando, the popular TV host, but then just five months before the planned wedding, Jill was shot dead in broad daylight. It was never solved. He thereby became compromised. Dr. S., Kate's baby doctor, is being sued by a former patient in High Court for over £300,000 for medical malpractice and clinical negligence. Would you want these two to deliver your baby? 'That's not something Kate or William have to worry about since neither of these doctors will be delivering anything except fake delivery news.'[37] All three children of William and Kate were recorded as delivered in St Mary's Hospital in Paddington. A letter signed by these suspect doctors was mounted on a wooden easel and displayed close to the gates of the palace for public view.

Figure: Diana and Kate: the two princesses wore the same sapphire ring.

---

[37] helpfreetheearth.com/news832_kate.html - deleted.

7

William and the Death of Thomas Kingston

Thomas Kingston was everything you might hope from an upper-crust British aristocrat. Known for his 'remorseless optimism' he was a devout Christian, cheerful, rich and good-looking, plus he had a beautiful wife. Then out of the blue we're told that he commits suicide. We're not even informed of the cause of death.

His father-in-law Prince Michael of Kent is a Freemasonic Grand Master, of the Grand Lodge of Master Masons, who could well be the highest-ranking Mason in the UK; through his mother he was a first cousin to the late Prince Philip, Duke of Edinburgh.[38] His daughter, Lady Gabriella Windsor, Prince William's cousin, was happily married to Thomas Kingston.

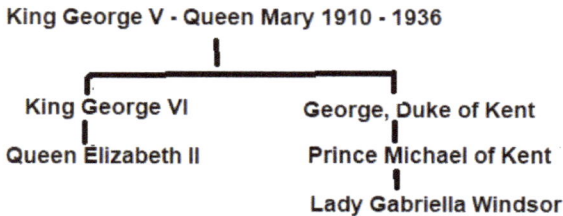

King George V - Queen Mary 1910 - 1936

King George VI	**George, Duke of Kent**
Queen Elizabeth II	**Prince Michael of Kent**
	Lady Gabriella Windsor

<u>Figure</u>: How lady Gabriella is related to the late Queen

Before the marriage, Thomas had been a boyfriend of Pippa, Kate's sister. He had been up on 'The Balcony' waving to us lot, the *hoi poloi,* down below. So, what happened? How come he did not enjoy some high level of protection? Why was his body cremated so fast? Whatever was happening to Kate, he would have known.

He died on 25 February, found dead of a 'catastrophic head wound' with a gun nearby. With one accord the papers all came out with the comment, 'Not a suspicious death ... no-one else was involved' – a remarkably absurd judgement. That kind of remark is supposed to emerge at the end of an investigation, not at the start, before it has even begun. He had been having lunch at his parent's posh manor house in Gloucestershire. His

---

[38] We don't really need this but: his mother Princess Marina of Greece was the niece of the Duke of Edinburgh's father, Prince Andrew of Greece.

father then took the dog for a walk. Half an hour later he returned and he and his wife began searching for their son. Eventually the father had to break into an outside shed that was locked and ... The papers all reported on how his son had "died from a catastrophic head wound," adding, "a gun was found beside the body". That was all anyone was going to tell us. A major friend of the royals and of Kate's family in particular gets bumped off, and no-one says a word.

Figure: Thomas Kingston and his wife lady Gabrielle Windsor

This event seems obscurely connected with what happened two days later, at a memorial service for William's godfather King Constantine, the last King of Greece, which took place at Windsor Castle. William was due to speak but abruptly cancelled his visit, pulling out at extremely short notice – an hour or so, literally - with no explanation. The parents of Gabriella, Thomas Kingston's wife, did attend that memorial service. It looks as if William could not face speaking at the event with them sitting right in front of him and why should that be? King Charles excused himself on the grounds that he was being treated for cancer. 'Curioser and curioser,' said Alice. That death on the 25th was not publicly reported until two days later - on Tuesday the 27th, at 6 pm - after the memorial service, which was held in the morning! Presumably Gabriella's family would have been told right away, and if so one is startled at them wanting to attend someone else's funeral service right after.

The ambulance call was put through at 6 pm – but that timing is too late, it just does not add up.

39

William and the Death of Thomas Kingston

Two days later, on the 29th, a news channel wondered, what would happen if Prince William were charged with a crime? Under the heading, 'What Happens to Prince Wiliam if he commits a serious crime?' it said, 'Prince William is believed to be one step away from landing in serious legal trouble' and explained that he "might be in legal trouble after allegedly manhandling his wife Kate Middleton."[39] Why were such vague insinuations being made about the future king of England? It hinted darkly that, "Prince William and the rest of the royal family continue to raise concerns over the internal affairs within the palace with a slew of suspicious moves," which would seem to allude to his having pulled out from the funeral of his godfather. The implication is being made, that these things are because of the sudden and unexplained death of Thomas Kingston.

Figure: The Kingstons with the royals

The silence around the Kingston death is comparable to that around Kate's disappearance. In both cases we must assume that the Palace is involved, for what else has the power to impose such deep silences? In the days after the death, close friends of Thomas Kingston came out to affirm that he had been in a happy mood and of sound mind.

Gloucester Coroner's Court opened its ultra-brief inquest into the death on March 1st, and curiously omitted mention of all the central issues: whose fingerprints were on the gun? Who owned it? Was the lock of the garden shed on the inside or outside? Was the cause of death an impact on the head, or a bullet? The report said that his mother went to search for

---

[39] Thenews.com by Web Desk, 'What happens to Prince William if he commits a serious crime?' 28.2.2024u

him, to see where he had got to, after which 'his father forced entry on a locked-out building when no reply could be gained.' Why did they believe their son was in the shed? None of that sounds very credible. Did his mother hear any sudden noise, if she was around the house? Were there any footprints around the dead body? Where was William at noon on the 25th of February? What about the bruise on his neck in the days afterwards? How come no members of the Kingston family were present at that Inquest, but only an official from the royal household? Why did no newspapers ask any of these questions?

A deep, deep silence reigned everywhere, with not a peep from any of the main characters. But tweets appeared on the 27th, the day of the memorial service, from royalty-watchers, which strangely synchronised with the announcement of the death.[40] These categorically affirmed that Prince William's absence from the service was unrelated to the mystery death two days earlier, thus:[41]

- It is important to note that this is NOT believed to be the reason why Prince William pulled out of today's memorial service' – Kate Mansey, 10 am on 27th

- Royal source says the death of Mr Kingston is NOT connected to the Prince of Wales's absence from King Constantine's memorial service today.' – Roya Nikkah, 10 am on 27th

etc. The *Daily Mail* gave its readers the same assurance. But those assurances, ostensibly designed to remove suspicion from William, served in fact to bring him into a central focus, for no-one had previously mentioned him in such a context. The only statement which appeared in all the papers, 'Not a suspicious death … no-one else was involved' clearly meant the opposite, that it *was* highly suspicious and others *had* been involved. Likewise these tweets seemed to mean the opposite, by persons highly constrained as to what they were allowed to say.

Persons acquainted with the main characters, or who for whatever reason had useful info to communicate, have one way of communicating it - given the general silence of friends, relatives, police, newspapers etc. -

---

[40] We follow the courageous and insightful lead of Murad Merali in his 'What happened to Thomas Kingston? Intense Deep dive Timeline.'
[41] Ibid at 3 mins.

namely by blog comments using an avatar. We here quote a few. Readers may wish to adopt a position of extreme scepticism, as the conclusions we might reach are liable to touch the very heir to the throne of England. In the days following, a bruise was seen on William's neck and a black eye on Tim Laurence, the husband of Princess Anne. Here is a comment by 'Dragonfly':

> At the funeral for Thomas the press photos showed princess Anne's husband with a black eye said to be from gardening, and William with bruising on face and neck. It was also stated that the afternoon before Thomas died, there was a party attended by Thomas and Gabriella, also other members of the royal family, what happened there that led to his death?

Another remarked that Princess Anne lived nearby: "I believe William and Anne's husband was there at the home of Tom's parents at Cotswalds, Anne's home is just up the road... Look into where Anne's husband was there, that day."

Here are a dozen more online comments, which could be helpful:

* 'What I found weird is the coroner's report did not say 'self-inflicted'. They are just letting people surmise that. It also does not anywhere say he was shot. It says 'traumatic head wound.' The fact there was a gun nearby means nothing. It could have been planted there or he may have had it in self- defence and was wrestled free of it. Guns are loud. I don't think he was shot.'

* 'Willboy has blood on his hands but his dad will cover, the way he did to his mother. Like father like son. Power, money tells everything.'

* 'Willy's personal matter for missing the funeral was probably his bruised face from something he did a couple days before.'

* 'On the day it happened Kingston's Father said he saw Prince William at the property that morning. That was never, ever, noted again.'

* 'William + Kingston were friends. I have even read that William was at the home that Sunday. In any case, the relationship was quite close - similar age, and Kingston's wife was quite close to William, too. As in they all hung out quite a bit.'

William and the Death of Thomas Kingston

* 'I heard that gathering was at Thomas Kingston's house and that William WAS there. Also, Princess Anne's husband (Sir Tim Laurence) was seen with a black eye when William had bruising. Was Sir Tim trying to break up a fight?'

* 'He was not shot, he was beaten in the head. I'm sure he didn't beat himself. So it can only be murder."

* 'Obviously, William has done something unusual. They're working too hard to clear his name without making direct accusations.'

* 'Something weird happened that week he died. Why did it take 2 days to report his death? What's with the bruises on Wm the day after the memorial he missed? Why did Princess Anne's husband also have a visible facial injury around that time? Why now, he [Thomas] was ex with Pippa, member of the RF, and good friends with Wm, and reportedly hanging out WITH Wm either the day before or earlier on the day he died. Like, it's just too many oddities to all be coincidence.'

* 'The bruises/hematomas on the side of W's neck are very alarming. In this area it's quite impossible to hit yourself, thus these injuries may have most likely been caused by battle.'

* 'I thought there were pictures of Willy and Thomas out drinking the night before Tom died.'

* 'Thomas Kingston Knew Too Much, So They Had To Silence Him!'

* 'Why did his wife Lady Gabriella move into Kensington palace? To be watched 24/7 so she doesn't talk to outside press?'

Some of the women ought to speak up - Anne, Pippa, Gabriella, they all must have their story? Prince Michael could be immune to being questioned, as a top freemason. Except for the king, royals are not immune from criminal investigation. The suicide hypothesis, which the media are endorsing, would make sense if and only if the fingerprints of Kingston were on the gun, which no-one has suggested.

Prince William and Anne's husband Tim Laurence emerge as primary suspects. In his schooldays William was known as 'Basher' Wills because of his temper, as being hot-headed and potentially violent. Concerning a club which the two brothers ran, 'Whenever trouble erupted, Harry invariably took the blame to protect the heir and conceal his explosive temper.'[42] Harry in *Spare* recalled such an outburst, during a dispute they were having as to whether Meghan was suitable for the RF. William grew furious and Harry backed away nervously:

> "It all happened so fast, so very fast. He grabbed me by the collar, ripping my necklace, and he knocked me to the floor. I landed on the dog's bowl, which cracked under my back, the pieces cutting into me. I lay there for a moment, dazed, then got to my feet and told him to get out."

William apologised and asked him not to tell Meghan. Thus, he has a sudden temper which can be uncontrollable. William is surely under a stressful condition, where he doesn't say very much. Growing up with his parents Charles and Diana airing their various affairs and grievances in public was a perfect nightmare.

He has to keep silent about the dark secrets of his family and has he not now become one of them? To whom can he speak? It was bad enough with everyone wondering where his wife had got to. Thomas Kingston might have been the only true friend that he was close to.

After these events, William went quiet and maybe was receiving some anger-management counselling. Presumably this incident will remain

---

[42] Tom Bower *Revenge* p.113.

unresolved, which could leave a future King William wide open to blackmail.

In June, Thomas Kingston's Wiki page vanished: his memory erased, he becomes an 'unperson' ...

What happened to Anne?

Princess Anne suffered a concussion to the head on June 23rd which put her in hospital for five days. She lacks any memory of the event, which is surmised to be due to a horse. There don't seem to have been any witnesses. Anne can only say that she remembers nothing but her head is badly bruised. As a lifelong equestrian, she would know never to get behind a horse where one can get kicked. Emerging from hospital she is still shaky and having to cancel appointments: even just a date for a summer barbeque had to be cancelled. But she did manage appointments scheduled for the end of August.

A couple of blog comments could be helpful:

- The only one in that family with a conscience in Princess Anne, and look what happened to her. Attacked at her own residence (allegedly) and is now (allegedly) suffering from loss of memory. BTW no one saw Anne enter or leave that hospital.

- The situation with Princess Anne is reminiscent of the situation with princess Catherine. Both entered and exited hospitals without being seen.

8

Kate: her Magic Re-appearance

'Kate "May Never Come Back" in Royal Role We Remember, Source Says'
'Celebrity News', June 4th

Christmas 2023 was the last real appearance of Princess Kate before her strange vanishing from public view. Her family business had imploded a few months earlier, with debts amounting to over two million: it had been a good-time holiday concept, taking out loans on the strength of their daughter having become a royal. William and Kate had been together for twelve years. In the deep silence following her disappearance, rumours grew, for example that William was having an affair with the married former model Rose Hanbury and they'd had a love-child, which led to Kate deciding to leave. Or to a row where William beat her, causing her to be carried away in an ambulance.

On the 28th of December an ambulance, escorted by police cars, left Sandringham where the royal couple had spent Christmas. It left at night-time, at 8.30 p.m. Later on we were told it was for a 'planned abdominal surgery,' but no ambulance would have been required for that. An ambulance trip means an emergency. William went to visit her, or at least was seen visiting the hospital – three weeks after her arrival! It was the King Edward VII hospital and he only paid that one visit on January 18th - and we have no evidence that he saw her there. She spent the whole month of January there, we were told. Ditto for Charles who likewise visits that hospital *once* during that month of January. Apart from those two, none of her friends or relatives came to visit. Journalists camping around the gates saw nothing. Was she really there? Or, if not, who was deceiving the British people in so cruel a manner? The narrative ceases to make any sense from this point on.

The hushed-up story of the hacking of Kate's medical records appears around the time of the ambulance departure. It has been greatly censored, but it seems that three employees of the Edward VII hospital were being investigated, for trying to access her medical record. We'd surely like to see what was on that record, but it's all hush-hush.

Kate's 42nd birthday on January 9th 2024 should have been a big occasion, as the future Queen of the Realm. But we heard nothing, nobody even saw a birthday cake. Normally her sister Pippa would post birthday greetings but not this year. Nothing disturbed the deep silence. Did the Palace tell Kate's family something the rest of us don't know?

Royal pundits did not seem to have heard about the three royal offspring being back at Berkshire's prestigious Lambrook school. Could that be, because at school they would be asked about their mother?

On the 17th of January, the Palace told us that Kate had undergone planned abdominal surgery, and that we should not expect to see her until after Easter. That seemed a long time to recover, some said. As the months ticked by, William would now and then assure us that she was recovering.

On the 28th, a Spanish journalist reported that Kate was in a medically-induced coma and her life was 'in grave danger,' claiming to have an inside source. The nanny of the Kate-William family is from Spain which lent some credibility to the tale. The story was categorically denied, then on the next day, as if in response, it was announced that Kate had been returned to her home - Adelaide cottage at Windsor - though we saw nothing.

Within weeks of these events, it was announced that both Sarah Ferguson and the King had cancer. Charles had two years to live, they reckoned. Plans were underway for his funeral. Some felt that this doom-laden cluster of royals-with-cancer was psychologically preparing us for the NHS's new anti-cancer jab.[43]

In February, members of Kate's family complained that they had not been told about the operation. On the 27th, William was due to attend the memorial service of his godfather King Constantine and make a speech there, but he pulled out abruptly (Chapter 7). That was only announced on the day, with no explanation.

The month of March saw no less than *five* phantom appearances of Kate. Who could thus be wishing to delude the British public?

---

[43] The NHS England will be the 'first health care system in the world to roll out the seven-minute injection' for cancer: england.nhs.uk/2006/08. It 'slashed treatment time by 75%.'

Kate: her Magic Re-appearance

5 March – 'Kate' plus mother in a car, driving near Windsor.

10 March   A family photomontage of a euphorically happy Kate + kids, 'taken by William.'

11 March Kate, so dark as to be hardly visible, was in a car beside William

16 March A young girl plus boyfriend on a farm near to the Windsor home are filmed prancing along, not greatly resembling Kate or William.

22 March An AI 'Kate' on a park bench reveals that she's got cancer.

Thereby we were being introduced to our frightening new AI future, where seeing is not believing. For intelligent discussion one had to turn to the Web, while the printed media just report what they are told – a key feature of this 21st century. Who on Earth is creating these fakes and why would they do them so *badly*? And how does William feel, being thus impersonated, even as he has to keep reassuring us that Kate is getting better, etc?

In the March 5th image, a woman with a heavily-jowled round face appears sitting next to Kate's mother in the front of a car. Opined one blogger, 'The photo in the car is Pippa, Kate's sister. I don't know how anyone could mistake this photo for Kate.' The four wheels of the car are visible, then in the background on the road behind the car are another two wheels!

On the next day Kate's uncle Gary Goldsmith just happened to be present on Big Brother. Asked the inevitable 'Where's Kate?' he replied

evasively that she was 'getting the best care in the world' and that the family would tell us, 'in due time.'

On Mother's Day March 10th, a heavily-edited image appeared of Kate and kids, which generated so much derision that 'Kate' had to issue an apology the next day! Various AI insertions were evident. If Kate was grievously unwell, how come those in the photo were all beaming with delight? Who was making fun of the British people by so evident a fake? Components of the image had been derived from an event of the previous November featuring Kate and her kids: the same clothes, the same boots, plus the face of Kate had been taken from a *Vogue* cover from a few years previously.

Figure: The *Telegraph* is shocked by fiddled photo

Multiple editing was evident from its metadata: a timestamp from March 8th then another the day after. Associated Press pulled the image saying they did not trust it: 'AP does not use digitally altered images' and they put a 'kill' notice upon it, meaning all copies had to be deleted. Other international picture agencies refused to distribute the doctored photo, claiming 'The source [i.e. the Palace] has manipulated the image.' Who could be responsible? How come large corporations were undermining the credibility of the Palace, a thing unheard-of?

Let's hear some baffled blog comments:

- 'What's strange is that the edited photo is so bad that it's like they wanted us to notice it was edited.'

- She looks 10 years younger in that Mother's Day mock-up ... a picture of health, not someone who looks so unwell they don't want to be seen.

Figure: Can you spot Kate, darkly in the background?

The next day, March 11, 'Kate' issued her apology, saying she just liked playing around with images. Then, as if trying to calm people down, another pic of her and Wills is released on that day, even more dubious, with Kate so dark as to be almost invisible. Her silhouette can just about be seen. It was found to have been taken from an old 2016 picture of her. A brick wall appeared conspicuously through the car windows which seemed too bright, while above the car appears quite faintly a different-looking brick wall; a discrepancy which seemed to be as senseless as the six car-wheels in the earlier fake Kate pic.

On the 16th of March, a video of what looked like a 19-year-old girl was seen jumping and bouncing along, taller than Kate and carrying a bag of shopping – hardly looking like a woman aged 42 recovering from major surgery. She and her bloke were on a farm somewhere around Windsor. Even George Galloway, famous for avoiding all 'conspiracy theories,' discussed on his 'Mother of all Talk Shows' the identity of the young girl.

A Mr 'Nelson Silva' had taken the video, claiming 'Digital Communications' hired him to do it. Watching the couple choosing loaves of bread in the farm shop, he thought he had seen them before somewhere. 'TMZ' posted the video, this being a news company that celebs work with. *The Sun* paid £200k to use it.

Figure: Farm shop video, of extra-young Kate

Scoffing comments appeared, eg: -

- 'No one who had major ab surgery wears tight skinny pants and walks like this. After ab surgery people walk different, carefully, slower….If she is so healthy and looks that good, why isn't she back at work for weeks and weeks?...

- That "Kate " has a wig, it looks so undone.

- …this woman is walking ahead of the future king. Kate does not.

- It's AI. Just before the 8 sec point, her foot is disconnected from her leg (play at .25 speed)

- "these Kate sightings are getting dumber and dumber"

- "I use to live near Windsor, there is hysteria around sighting royals- if Kate was grocery shopping with William not only would they be mobbed-there would have been a hundred pictures uploaded."

A lady who worked at the farm explained that, whenever a royal came there, they made sure the whole area was shut down, but on the said day the supposed Kate was seen at the farm, the area was never shut down, it was business as usual, which means it was not Kate.

News articles had initially reported that the royal couple were seen on the farm and these came out with no videos. Then the next day this blurry vid appeared. The BBC was careful to use 'reportedly' and 'allegedly' when describing it.

The AI Simulation

A week later, on the 22nd of March, AI itself spoke to us. We've entered a new world, when a digitally-fabricated 'princess' image can speak to the British people, *as if it were real,* deceiving them over a matter of life and death. Anyone could see the optical illusion, with Kate sitting more or less in the middle of the bench, with three slats visible on one side, and five on the other. Escher would have approved.

Sceptics noted how the slats were of different sizes and spaces on either side of 'Kate' - in no way due to perspective. Blogs discussing this would vanish. The weather had been cold that March, and Nature was *not* in bloom, despite what was shown on the totally unmoving green-screen in the background. Would someone recovering from surgery really sit outside without a coat? The park bench appeared shiny enough to reflect the pattern of the stripey top that 'Kate' was wearing. Her right arm appeared flat and two-dimensional, her left shoulder wasn't right..

Figure: AI construct of 'Kate' on a Bench in Windsor Gardens

Slowing down the vid and looking at her hands, the wedding-ring is seen to appear and disappear. Hands are always difficult for AI to get right. Her face is an AI construct as shown by the two dark lines on either side of it, plus her long neck and the lines on it don't look right. Getty images released an editor's note stating that the video 'may not adhere to its editorial policy' and that the clip was provided by a 'third party organization,' the 3rd party in this instance being the BBC (Gettyimages, Editor's Note, 22 March 2024)

Figure: AI version of Kate's ring, on park bench video, which vanishes and re-appears (for slow speed, choose 'Settings' => 'Playback speed' => 0.25).[44]

The date of 22 March is regarded as being 'Skull and Bones Day' because that US secret society has its Lodge number 322. The various Kate-simulation images thus culminated on this date.

We were told it was filmed in Windsor Gardens, but it turned out that no benches there resembled the one shown. A tweet was entitled 'Found the bench the video was supposedly shot on at Windsor Gardens. There is NO WAY it's the same bench.' It explained:

The video was definitely recorded at Windsor Gardens. If you google benches there, these are the only benches that look remotely close to the one in the video. My opinion is that there was an AI prompt to generate a video in the gardens on one of these benches and AI generated this video. Close, but not nearly close enough.

The AI figure on the bench averred that Kate had not been seen because she had got cancer. No-one has ever heard of a person diagnosed as having cancer who therefore vanishes from view. It just is not that kind of illness. Is she supposed to be staying in her cottage or hospital, all day every day? The King and Fergie have likewise been so diagnosed but that has not stopped them from being seen.

In March the British Army removed a post saying Kate would be attending their annual event on June 8th this year, a week before the

---

[44] Youtube, BLUX: 'Kate Middleton: Further AI proof: the ring, the eyes, the hair.'

trooping of the colour, in her capacity as Honorary Colonel of the Irish Guards. She would normally be in a carriage procession, with William and Charles riding on horseback beside her, down Horse Guards Parade. The glorious ritual and pageant that only England could provide was all there and waiting, but ... no Kate.

The Queen's will left 110m dollars' worth of jewellery to Kate, which could be a dangerously large amount, as regards the life of the person receiving it.

The children of Kate remained largely unseen. Only George appeared as William took him out a couple of times to watch football. The other two remained unseen since Xmas and why might that be? One view would be, that William does not want journalists to quiz his kids about whatever has happened to their mother. He took one of them, George, to a football match which was feasible, there being enough noise and excitement that no such opportunity could arise.

Bloggers were heard ruminating upon the deep silence, the senseless illusions:

- "Kate is gone. William and Rose are to be blamed. There is so much darkness about what has happened to Kate. If they could produce Kate, they would. Now I believed she is either dead or beyond help. No fairy tale happy ever after ending for her. She was never in that hospital. Why can't her family speak up?"

- "When the Queen was there, there was consistency, now they are up and down like a yo-yo. The media is running out of lies. Whatever is happening with Kate has to do with what happened with Thomas Kingston ... a suicide, but the gun was found nowhere near his hand/body. Same circle."

The Magic Re-appearance

Most unexpectedly, Kate sprung back at a mere 24 hours-notice, not looking in the slightest like a cancer treatment patient, but younger and

Figure: Two fake 'Kate's? 22 March, then 15 June

more radiant than ever. Every single front page around the world carried the picture. A new Queen of Hearts show was up and running! Here was the strange sequence:

June 2024

13th William pays a 'private' visit to MI6
14th Kate's reappearance at Trooping of the Colour is announced
15th Trooping of the Colour

Thereby hangs a tale, to be sure, but no-one is likely to tell us about it! Did William have to confirm with Britain's secret service that the new Kate-clone would be up and running by the 15th?

It's a very good double, if so it is. Here to remind you is 'real Kate' as last seen, Christmas day 2023.

Figure: Yes, this is the lovely **real Kate** on Xmas day 2023!

In contrast, here 'Kate' is at *Trooping*, inside her royal carriage. Commented 'Annabella's intuition' on this image, 'Are we supposed to believe this is the 42-year old Katherine Middleton who has had three children and been though gruelling cancer treatment? C'mon!' Adding 'You can tell, her face is round, it's not oblong, it's a round head... Also her ears stick out, the real KM her ears did not stick

out at all. Her forehead is shorter.[45]

Soon the internet was heaving with conspiracy theories. To be sure, nothing made sense. As before, we quote from a few bloggers, wrestling with the mystery. Bloggers are like the chorus of a Greek tragedy: after the main characters speak their parts, then in response the chorus is heard, often a lamentation, expressing popular sentiment.

I suggest not trying to form an opinion on this matter, but rather keep an open mind:

- She doesn't have bloody cancer. At best, she had cosmetic surgery because she has never looked so young, even when she was young. At worse, it wasn't even her, or at least not the original.

---

[45] Youtube Anabella's Intuition, 'Real Kate was not at Wimbledon in 2024' (deleted). 'Lifelike AI clone sits though business interview' on foxbusiness.com 9.8.24 shows co-founder of the company Delphi with his 'clone' next to him, both answering questions.

- for a lady doing chemo and feeling weak, she sure does wear very high heels.
- 'someone' looks SO much younger.
- If chemo treatment was so beautifying on women, Princess Catherine has just launched a new beauty routine which would surpass ozempic! Wake up people! Another doppelganger!
- 10 million to celebrate a birthday when his birthday is in November? Instead of slimming down the monarchy, slim down the unnecessary second birthday celebrations.
- Her clothes are the same as Audrey Hepburn in the film 'My Fair Lady' - where she's taught to become another version of herself and play a new character!!
- That was her. This is what happened. William beat the breaks off of Kate back in December and she got plastic surgery and did some work simultaneously she looks tucked.
- Piers Morgan said that what he heard was horrible news about Princess Catherine. William must have done a number on her face. I think she had to have a facelift to correct the damage to her face.
- Tom Bower did say Kate's absence was to do with her face and that it was very serious.
- Let's talk about the eyebrow scar everyone's talking about, which was not there when she went to church at Christmas.
- We can't believe the images anymore.
- The face lift theory is wrong. It only takes 2 months to recover from swelling and bruises. Makeup does the rest. She has been out of the public eye for 6 months, so obviously, something else is going on.
- Lots of red flags at the Trooping of Colours, Kate replaced barely spoke with William, she also walked ahead of him at a certain point, her stroking of Charlotte's hair seemed a bit unlike the real Kate, she barely interacted with Louie unlike other engagements, that was not the real Kate.

- if Kate did make her first real appearance at Trooping, then where was her "birth family"? Surely, they would have been there in support?

- All I'm saying is that almost all of the footage was poor quality. Grainy, blurring, out of focus and not well zoomed in, as if the pics were meant to be kept at a distance. Was so noticeable. Everyone's instincts are telling them something is wrong. We may not know what but instincts are never wrong. The powers that be are hoping that everyone stays 'dumbed down'. I used to love the time of Diana and they were people we admired. Now it's just downright sinister you can feel it in all their pics etc

- No one's reported on how/where Kate is getting her cancer treatment, which takes dozens of medical professionals, labs, equipment, blood tests, fusion tubes, etc. All at home?? Anyone seen a medical van coming or going?

- I think William's visit to M16 the day before Trooping was to get him to officially sign off on the final production. I think as days go by, we will start gathering more clues as to what technologies they are capable of!

- Most people saw it on telly or net, not in person, so you can't swear that was the real her. Plus, AI is merged with the real person's image to work, all you need is a lookalike playing the part then you lay the program on top. The footage shows missing limbs & glitching, & the blurred skin texture always seen in AI,[46] that's why she looked younger & less stringy!!

- I've been seeing Catherine since she arrived at the royals. I don't think she had cancer at all, I think she was gone for over 6 months because she and William were having marriage problems. William will never leave his mistress Rose because they were lovers before he married Catherine. He's exactly like his father. Also, the photos of Catherine when she was in the carriage with her children. She

---

[46] youtube.com/watch?v=wUyempTKyl4 Murad 17.6.24

looked upset then she smiled. She didn't once wave to the crowd, which was very strange. This could be a hoax to distract the public.

- The real one is gone, this is a clone. A clone takes 6 months to be ready and they've to be replaced every 6 months or 3 years if it's a good one. Charlotte and Louis too. William took them out. That's the reason she looks so young and refreshing. Wake people.

This one's my favourite:

- It is all extremely odd. I am sensing smoke and mirrors again. Each one of them. PW had a very distant look like he was not focusing on anyone's face. Almost like AI. Catherine looked very beautiful and glowing but again shifting, one minute plastic next minute human. Charlotte, George and Louis looked worried and frowning a lot. Less attached to their family and strange somehow. Charlie looks different every time he is pictured. I think his look alike was working overtime. Cammie, well she just looked very old, a wrinkled prune. Aging fast. Maybe the magic formula to keep her young is no longer available.

It's hard to see how Kate can ever be allowed out to mingle with ordinary people – who would at once demand answers about the bizarre sequence of stories we've all been put though. Where had they come from? Was it her apologising after the weird AI construct put out on Mother's Day? Will she please explain the message that echoed in headlines around the world on June 4th,

'Kate "May Never Come Back" in Royal Role We Remember'

– which had seemed so final, as if she were really gone? If she looked so lovely and healthy when she did re-appear, how could that bulletin have been released a mere ten days earlier? Also, cancer sufferers battling with chemotherapy have expressed surprise at the way she 'comes out looking like she's had a face lift, boob job, new teeth etc' - they wondered whether she had been using 'cancer' merely as a cover to recover from these plastic surgeries? One appreciates the royal motto 'Never explain, never apologise' and yet – we need her story!

9

A Game of Tennis

The real Kate seemed to turn up on the last day of Wimbledon on July 13th, didn't she? Here she is:

You do believe that's her, don't you? She received a large standing ovation, gracefully gave out the prizes, and was accompanied by her daughter Charlotte. Despite being frail and thin, everyone said she looked fine. William was far away. Was that not the first real, definite appearance of the woman who was Kate, six months after she'd vanished at Christmas?

As with the previous 'appearance' at Trooping, we were only told that she would be appearing, on the day before. Then, on the day after, we were informed that she had no further engagements planned for the rest of the year, she will be 'on holiday.' On holiday from what? What work had she ever done? There was a feeling of being betrayed, at not getting to see the

A Game of Tennis

future Queen of England again, for the forseeable future.

As before, we turn to insightful blog comments for guidance –

[The kids are] home schooled so they can't tell the truth. Willy lives elsewhere, Kate is questionably Kate. They brought out 3.0 and are putting her away for the summer.

That was not Kath it was a double. Willy and Kath are not going on holidays he keeps pushing on with dates in case he get caught for Kath's demise.

It must be hard work watching tennis.

Kate and William is happy living the laziest life they wanted.

Glad you're starting to see why we think she doesn't have cancer - I don't know if it was her idea to lie, but she damn sure isn't speaking up. I guess they are in too deep now.

That's nice, after a stressful day of William attending a football game and Kate attending Wimbledon, they need to take a break and relax. I doubt the two of them will be spending the summer together.

William and Kate have been on holiday all year! If they got payed a salary per hour work they would be paupers! Lol both are absurd.

She was at neither Trooping nor Wimbledon. Got to pull back the doubles now, give them a rest before people really begin to wake up.

We actually don't really know if the real Kate was actually the one at TOTC and Wimbledon. She certainly looks younger and fresher than real Kate used to be before Dec last year.

Her fingers need a much-needed break from editing photos and lying to the world.

I wonder what repliKate whispered to Lleyton Hewitt. He went completely red in the face. Dailymail has pictures of it.

Inevitably, comparisons are made with Our Princess, by no means forgotten:

Lady Diana was humble, respectful, sweet, and Adorable.

Plus, this post was made on Camilla's birthday:

Was not aware that Horse's Birthdays are celebrated. With Hay in muddy fields.

Deep was the silence of our Kate. She had in fact nothing to say, no word of greeting. After the strange six months of fabricated images of her, would she not wish to explain who she is and what has been happening to her? What is her story? Are there no words from her own mouth to tell us how she is? What does she do every day in her home, never seen by us, the public, and what does she intend to be doing for the rest of this year when she will not be seen? Could she not have managed just a few words to some adoring *Royalty* journalist? She had been so extravert for years and now, suddenly, cannot be seen?

Once this year we did get to see a real, speaking Kate. It happened at Wimbledon, on the last day, when she spoke of her own accord. Sitting in the royal box, she turned to address a tennis champ sitting right behind her, Lleyton Hewitt. On a previous year she had presented him with a tennis award. Her remarks made him turn bright red with embarassment, he 'became red-faced' as Kate whispered something to him. *Daily Mail* pictures showed the startled and flustered champ. That is hardly how we would have expected Kate to behave.

As before, let's hear a few blog-comments. A warning, some of these are entertaining the idea that a clone has been produced:

As soon as I heard that she revealed something to Lleyton I thought he better have great security protection.

Perhaps the fake did not know something Lleyton Hewitt mentioned to her, bear in mind the real Catherine had previously presented him with a trophy when he won Wimbledon...perhaps the copy wasn't programmed to know that, and he realised it's not her.

Another reader confirmed what you have just said about her telling Hewitt she was not the real Kate.

I wonder how Bec, Lleyton's wife felt about all the whispering. It was so odd.

So Kate is not scheduled to make any more appearances this summer. I'm sure the palace is concerned when she went rogue and the episode that happened with Hewitt. I really hope Hewitt says something to the media about her revelation to him.

For a man to go so beetroot red whatever was said had to be very personal, having revealed she was an imposter she then must have propositioned him somehow.

Was the real Kate flirtatious and did this version forget she is married? Or does this version have an understanding that she is no longer married?

Well this hide and seek cannot go on forever.

Princess Catherine wouldn't do that, only if she was manic.

The new Kate is an 'it'.

One senses, in the above comments, a feeling of betrayal, of abandonment and even of trickery. Princess Catherine received a rapturous response at Wimbledon, with a prolonged standing ovation and cheering crowds whenever she was seen … then she was gone. There is a sense of royalty no longer caring about us, which also manifests in the Palace's new habit of putting out staged, photoshopped pictures.

Figure: Kate's children watching on TV the football final, 13th July?

A Game of Tennis

A picture from the Palace showed the *backs* of two of Kate's children watching the football match in Germany, on the *same day* as the Wimbledon final, a match attended by their father. Why would we be shown their backs? Who would want another image of Charlotte, on the same day in which she had done very well appearing with her mother? Web-sleuths soon decided it was yet another photoshopped op: 'No sooner did we see the real Kate swanning around at Wimbledon with the real Charlotte, then Kensington Palace were back to trolling us with photoshopped / AI images.'[47]

They felt that the arms of the children weren't right, especially the arm in the middle which seemed 'chopped off.' The sunlight illuminating them was too high in the sky for the late evening when England won the game, which they're supposedly watching. Royalty-watchers were irked:

> And then the further implications of their continued use of Ai. Today it is kids watching football. Tomorrow, it could be future official visits they can't be bothered to go to.

> AI will give the lazy royals a chance to do even less. It's reassuring that the kids have been seen publicly. But what a future for them in the world they're growing up in. The twilight world of fakery, lies and obfuscation.

> Thinking out loud...pre-Kate's December 2023 "disappearance", did the palace ever post these types of weird faceless pics of various members of the RF with their backs to the camera? Or is this a completely new phenomenon in the past few months?

Yes, it is.

The idea that a young child would spend the day watching tennis and then choose to spend the evening watching a game of football on TV, is just absurd. Why would anyone dream up such a thing? then, have you ever

---

[47] 'Royal appearances now by AI,' KMM (Kate Middleton Missing) online community – reddit.com/r/KateMiddletonMissing/comments/1e54dii/royal_appearances_now_by_ai_the_charlotte_and/

heard of two children wearing T-shirts with their names printed on the back? As if their parents couldn't remember which was which?

People were wondering, why didn't 'Kate' just photograph her real two kids? This was but the latest in a string of fabricated pictures where we don't know what the point is and maybe there was none: unless, perchance, to dissolve the bond of trust which the British people used to have towards their royal family.

To be reminded of what the real Kate used to be like, try listening to her lecture, 'The Princess of Wales' speech at the *Shaping Us* National Symposium.' It was a wise and warmly inspiring talk. It was given in September of 2023 – a *mere three months* before the Vanishing. Let's hear a few of the blog-comments:

> Wonderful speech, good crowd, classy orator. She just exudes class, compassion and selflessness.

> I have never lost sight of Catherine since the day she wed Prince William. After all these years, I couldn't be more proud of her. Her stoicism, far sightedness, emotional intelligence, maturity, and unwavering focus on her family, projects and work is remarkable.

> Couldn't be prouder of my Princess. Her genuine care and passion shine through,

etc. Would we want to have such a person as queen of England? Yes indeed, I suggest that we truly would. But, do we have that option, is she still around?

I sometimes feel that the soul of Kate has been uploaded into the Borg or the Matrix. Just as you've finally convinced yourself that she really doesn't exist anymore, then lo, a new Kate 4.0 will appear, with much fanfare and adoring journos …

September 9th

A happy-family video is released, from their home in Norfolk. The *Daily Mail* called it 'an outpouring of intimacy' which some felt was excessive (10

September) then a couple of days later the *Mail*'s Stephen Glover came out with an article entitled: 'if William and Kate want to feed us a fairytale, I feel disaster may follow.' But still, let us murmur, *no-one has seen Kate*, she has not appeared anywhere.

A video has been released, that is all, which affirms that she is over her 'preventative chemotherapy' cancer treatment. She looks fine, radiantly happy, having not lost a hair of her head from the gruelling chemo treatment which so badly afflicts other mortals. Nor have we seen any sign of any cancer-treatment equipment or which hospital she visited or gratitude to any team of nurses or doctors. Her sapphire ring from Diana is gone.

Most people seem to have enjoyed it, thus here is one comment:

> Everything about her has always defined grace, courage, inspiration, tenacity, patience, loyalty and love. She is the best of us.

Indeed, let us hope so. But, others felt that things were not quite right. As we've noted before, for this story – *of our future queen* – one searches for insight in the blog comments -

> That was the most shmoltzy video I've ever seen. It's reminiscent of an ethereal Tarot card reader and soo unlike anything Kate would ever say.

> That photo shoot was: cringy, embarrassing, awkward, disingenuous, pretentious, unnatural, fake, weird and bizarre.

> I was waiting to see if Julie Andrews was going to pop out singing "the hills are alive with the sound of music."

> I have NO idea HOW Kate MADE William do this ridiculously phony, disingenuous video, but SHE DID.

> The video was absolutely cringe; the portion with her head placed on his shoulder was so inauthentic - it was so clearly choreographed; it was very sad.

> The video felt like a memorial tribute to Kate!

> If you're gonna be open, tell us what kind of cancer you have Kate.

> Where was Kate's 'shunt' placed? Cancer patients have them to receive

chemo, either arm or chest, where's Kate's? We've seen her upper arm and now chest, where is it? She never had cancer.

She looks younger and healthier. How can that be after a chemo? For me, the scene that stands out is the field scene (like in the Gladiator movie). Like she is in heaven/afterlife. Is she really dead?

Unfortunately Kate can't come to the phone right now. THAT is why Videos are coming in so handy...

I don't believe they were up-to-date photos. The kids looked younger than they are now.

Notice they are not all wearing the same clothes throughout the video.

WHY can't they sit down for an interview? Why?

They're destroying her name, so nobody is going to miss her or want anything from her...the plan is fulfilled.

Prayers to Princess Catherine, b/c IMO that's not her and I've believed that for a long long time??

Is it really Kate? IMO, it is a doppelganger used to cover up a crime equivalent to the death of Diana.

This is an old video. Their dog LUPO who is featured died years ago, do they think we are THAT dumb?

Finally in October we see her she returning into the light of day. No-one will explain anything. For a 'planned abdominal surgery' the previous December one would expect her to *visit* the hospital, not be taken at night in an ambulance accompanied by a police car. One hears of such a scenario for people being 'sectioned,' i.e. forcibly taken with or without consent to a hospital (under the Mental Health Act.) and given drugs.

A journalist known to the author was in Germany having 'dendritic cell cancer treatment' which is not allowed in the UK but a lot of people believe it is effective. He was speaking to a doctor who let it slip out, almost by accident, that Kate had come to Germany for such cancer treatment. That would make sense – one would certainly not expect the King to approve of chemotherapy. Were she actually out of the country for maybe nine months of 2024, that could explain quite a lot.

9

No Heirs for the Spare

The children of Meghan Markle are in a different category from those of Kate Middleton. Kate's do really exist.

It's not my business to judge Prince Harry and the awful damage he has inflicted upon his fellow-royals. I'm merely stating that he has no royal kids. He has followed a course whereby his life has to be based upon astounding dishonesty and he sees no other option. No two little kids of his are running around his luxury pad in California. After he and Meghan were given a wedding paid for by British taxpayers, the maverick royal couple were soon heard complaining about everything – mainly the British media and the royal family – as a pretext to scoot off to America and renounce British citizenship. As Lady C. (who has written the weighty tome about the royal couple[48]) well stated, Meghan Markle is 'a dominating hustler whose game plan is that of a lone wolf operative pretending to be a farm animal.' Lady C. is quite quotable, here's another from her about the fake pregnancy: 'When MM's own father and her 2nd husband Trevor[49] both tell the same story of MM having a hysterectomy [as she had uterine damage, due to abortions, N.K.] then I do tend to believe she is incapable of delivering an infant.' That's it folks, she hasn't got a womb.

In her impressive upper-crust language, Lady C. laid down her judgement, that Meghan should

'provide the proof to the world that those children were born in such a way that no questions can be asked, which means they have to provide absolute proof that Meghan bore those children and was delivered of those children herself... If they can't do that, those children should be removed from the line of succession forthwith.'

---

[48] Lady Colin Campell, *Meghan and Harry: The Real Story*, 2024.
[49] Trevor Engelston, her second husband, lasted 16 months: they divorced in 2013. As a student she was briefly married to a fellow college student at Northwestern University studying law, Joe Giuliano. His parents objected to her so it had to be anulled. He became a practicing lawyer in Chicago. She bore him a daughter, now in her twenties.

No Heirs for the Spare

Hear, hear! MM displayed no pregnancy symptoms nor did any of her actions show her to be pregnant: no visits to clinics, no doctors arriving. This would be a fairly high-risk pregnancy, for a woman conceiving in her late 30s. Immediately after announcing it at Princess Eugenie's wedding, (October 2018) they then flew off to Australia. Would a pregnant woman, especially at that age, really choose to do that?

Once more we quote the perceptive Lady C., that 'Since 1936 always the Home Secretary has witnessed the birth' of a royal child', so that no 'bastard' could accede to the throne unjustly: 'The arrival of these two children [of Meghan] has been cloaked with cloak and dagger secrecy.' The monarchy has to be governed by law and custom and protocol, with the law of succession stating that the heir must come 'from the body of the lawful wife of the blood-royal.' No adopted child can be in the line of succession (Royal Marriages Act and 2005 Embryology Act) and only a natural-born child of a husband and wife can succeed to the throne.

She would always be photographed holding her belly while 'pregnant' which pregnant women don't do; probably to ensure the 'bump' didn't drop down to her knees again.

Figure: bump or no bump?

Many found Harry's written account of Archie's birth to be absurd, especially the bit about "Within two hours of our son being born we were back at Frogmore." In her late thirties, did Meghan walk out of hospital hours after giving birth? (*Spare*, p365). Here are some of the incredulous comments:

- Nurses all say they don't believe the story.

- My retired Consultant Anaesthetist friend spat out her coffee in disbelief when she read that Meghan was let out of a hospital within 6 hours of giving birth after an epidural.

- The RF announcement of Lily's birth said "a daughter was born FOR the Duke and Duchess of Sussex", not TO. The palace knows all.

- The one thing that stands out for me is the lack of official birth certificates for either child

Did Meghan gave birth to Archie at Portland hospital in London on May 6? The Announcement on a mounted board in front of Buckingham palace did not include names of the two doctors, which prompted questions. Palace aides were unclear what was happening –

- "We were led to believe by palace aides that baby Sussex was born at Frogmore Cottage, but in fact he arrived at private London hospital the Portland," the *Sun* corr. wrote on Twitter.

- "The Portland Hospital is a bit of sleight of hand - look over here!! Portland Hospital doesn't make sense for a geriatric mother, with money. Portland doesn't have an emergency, doesn't have neonatal care if there are complications."

- It's plain to see that neither child resembles their "mother" at all!

- Not one doctor came forward to confirm the delivery.

- One day she's visibly pregnant, then the next as if she's hardly pregnant at all... She wore a fake pregnancy bump which kept expanding, contracting and moving.

Social media were buzzing with stories of fake pregnancies but no British newspaper would touch the topic. Just like Kate, Meghan had been wearing a silicone pregnancy-simulation kit. Portland hospital said it had no record of her being there.

In the famous interview, MM told Oprah she had not announced her birth because she did not want crowds of press. However it has been a condition of royal births for centuries, that they *have to be witnessed*. The Royal baby bulletin lacked the doctor's signature or details of where the birth took place.

Displaying the 'Archie' doll

On May 8th, 2019, two days after the alleged birth of Harry's first child, the royal couple were filmed in the chapel at Windsor Castle where they were married a year earlier, with Harry holding a well-wrapped up 'baby.' It remained immobile during the performance, showing no sign of life. Meghan by his side hardly touches it, but keeps patting Harry. They keep grinning at each other as they appear and walk down the aisle, which tends to suggest deception. Harry keeps glancing nervously at Meghan as if to say, Are you sure we can get away with this?

Figure: the doll 'Archie' is shown to the world

The doll's face is almost completely concealed, we don't even see an eyelid flutter. A journalist asks, 'Can we have a little peek at him? We can't quite see his face' – then the baby doll is turned ever so slightly *but* not enough to show the face. Harry tries to sound like a father but it comes out as totally fake:

> Everyone says the baby has changed so much over two weeks, we're basically monitoring how the changing process happens... we're just so thrilled to have our own little bundle of joy.

That was a major blunder, after it had supposedly existed for only two days. Meghan quickly corrects him, saying 'It's been a special couple of days.'[50]

---

[50] Watch the video at, e.g. *Trust NOT What Is Being Said, But What Your Eyes Are Telling You* by 'the Royal Grift.'

Harry may have fathered a bastard child four months into the marriage, and Meghan, who was unable to conceive, perceived an opportunity: they would agree to pay off the mortgage for the mother of 'Archie' if they could use her baby. We're shown Meghan with a one year old Archie reading a story.[51] She keeps smiling at the camera not looking remotely like a mother: we feel no bond between mother and child. The real mother, who lives in England, soon wanted it back.

Here are blogger comments, doubting the phantom kids:

- They jet all around the world with no sign of the kids, but talk nonstop about them.

- On the photo of 'Archie's' christening (6.7.19), the data showed the photo was taken on may 8th, 2 days after his supposed 'birth', he was definitely not 2 days old in that photo. Also he has always looked older than his age.

- [concerning 'Lilibet'] The Californian records of births, marriages and deaths have no record of her being born in California.

- No one in California has ever seen their kids... No photo in US showing them with her children.

- The state of California should be investigating if these children even exist and who do they actually belong to.

- Her kids' hair colour keeps changing: brown, black even red. Blurry pictures of dolls, kids-for-rent...First she produces a ginger head child completely white, followed up with a perfectly white, ginger daughter: given the geriatric pregnancy at her age having two perfect future titled children ... (brown is a dominant gene for hair colour). ALL formerly pregnant women KNOW it's IMPOSSIBLE to do what Megsy did while "pregnant."

- Pray tell how a child can go from a flaming redhead to a dark-haired boy in such a short time.

- "All old pictures we've seen over and over. Plus we never see their faces properly, unless they are pictures of them as babies or

---

[51] Search for video MM 'duck rabbit.'

toddlers. What about brand new pics of what they look like now, frontal pics?"

- "Wouldn't it have been nice to actually SEE THE CHILDRENS FACES instead of them always from behind?"

- "Why didn't she pose with the baby outside the hospital? For someone who is hungry for attention that was a huge red flag. "

- 'You can tell that MM has no connection to those kids. Whenever she has them, they don't hold her back and just kind of hang off of her, like she is a stranger. MM has absolutely no Mom Vibes whatsoever.'

- When they presented "Archie" in the hallway to the press, I was thinking at the moment: this is a doll... I realised that Archie wasn't hers, likewise for the photos of her clumsily holding him at that polo match! No mother holds her baby like that! I thought that she was about to drop him, tbh!

People have surmised that the couple have some art of 'conjuring a fabricated memory' while speaking in public. Locals wondered, at what school was Archie? No parents would comment upon their kids having seen him. Harry and Meghan were visible enough, but no youngsters were with them. Californians are heard discussing 'Archie sightings.'

"Weird to close off your kids to both sets of grandparents" was one comment. The royal couple had to do that, because their phantom kids could not be shown. Were MM to visit her father - who was complaining loudly about having been abandoned by her - he would surely have asked to see his grandchildren.

Various reports including one from Portland Hospital stated that the first child had been delivered by the distinguished Dr Penny Law, Countess of Bradford. However, her husband Richard Bradford soon tweeted that he and his wife had been away on vacation over that period: "My wife did not deliver, *The Sun* gave a false report."[52]

The child was called Archie Harrison but Archie is hardly a proper name

---

[52] 'Archie' birth on May 6, 2019: for claim that only a surrogate birth took place, see bookwormonthecase.co.za/letter-sent-to-the-archbishop/

for a man, being rather (one gathers) the informal term of endearment used for the young Prince George, Kate and William's son. They appropriated that, as they later took 'Lilibet', the Queen's private name, for their second child. 'Harrison' is not-so-subtly meant to remind us he's Harry's son.

Figure: put it down, Harry, it's not your kid

A former housekeeper at H&M's California estate, Mrs Maria Gonzales, has averred that Lilibet is her daughter. In late 2020 she became pregnant, then the royal couple prevailed upon her, offering a fee of $250k that was in essence a purchase agreement. She would carry the baby to term but her name would remain undisclosed on all legal documents and she would not seek a maternal relation post-birth. But, she found it difficult to adhere to that contract, and is now claiming to have DNA proof. She is white. She is not the first to lay claim to being the mother![53] The royal couple are of course denying this. Ms Gonzales should hand the money back, that's for sure.

For the Queen's Platinum Jubilee celebrations celebrating her 70 year reign, in 2022, Harry and Meghan flew in from LA, arriving at Farnborough airport on June 1st. Papers reported that the couple *plus their two children* were due to arrive. A car ordered by the Queen picked them up with their

---

[53] Los Angeles inhabitant Stassi Schroeder is said to allow her daughter Hartford to act as Lily, their second child, allegedly born 4 June 2021. Back up Rent-A-Kids are Heather Dorak's daughter for Lilibet and August Brooksbanks. Side-by-side photos of August and "Archie" are one and the same. The photographer used by H&M is Mr Missan Harriman who takes the fiddled photos.

two kids from the airport, averred the *Daily Mail*. A couple of days later, it was reported that the Queen had met the child Lilibet, though no photos showed this 'private' event. The *Mail* qualified its account using 'reportedly' and 'are said to.' Many were the glamorous photos of H&M during the celebrations, having no kids with them.

Their plane had flown in from LA on the evening of June 1st, when airport ground staff reported that the royal couple had arrived *without* any kids - there were no photos of the happy family. One report stated,

> "I was working as a security officer at the MOD site next to it. From what I heard no children were with him... No children were entered on the flight manifest. It's a legal requirement that all passengers, no matter how young, are entered on every flight manifest - even on a private flight."

Why would British newspapers allow themselves to be duped in this manner?

Are the royal couple a pair of complete, total liars or do they just live in a make-believe world? One thinks of Harry's endless talk about truth, etc. But, consider this: during the Oprah interview, Meghan commented upon how her baby 'Archie' had not been awarded a title of 'Prince' by the Royal family and that was due, she brazenly affirmed, to 'racism.' Let us put aside the fact that the pictures of her two little kids show them as both marble-white. The crystal-clear rule formulated by an earlier monarch, of which Harry and Meghan could not have been ignorant, states that grandchildren of the monarch get to be princes and princesses, but not great-grandchildren. It's not rocket science. While the old Queen was alive, the children of Harry and William could not acquire a royal title, however they could do that as soon as Charles became king. It had nothing to do with anyone's choice.

So that was quite a whopper. Americans believed it. In due course the two alleged offspring became Prince Archie and Princess Lilibet - the first time in history that royal titles were bestowed upon kids who don't actually exist.

Once Meghan made the 'racist' accusation, the RF could never really recover. No specific cases or events had been cited, so no-one could respond. Prince Harry followed through by damning the Commonwealth as a racist institution. Most people, at least most English people, would agree that the old Queen and her RF had done a fine job in the post-colonial era in endeavouring to keep the Commonwealth together on the basis of mutual trade, respect and friendship; in which respect the old queen was a most un-racist person, who had always gone out of her way to show respect towards the different people in the commonwealth countries.[54] The RF was looking forward to having a mixed-race person as part of the Firm, helping to solve the problem of their contemporary relevance. As the old Queen quipped, 'Mr Corbyn will find it much more difficult to get rid of us now that Meghan's in the family.'[55]

The couple soon became No 1 trending on social media. MM just sailed from one success to another, until 'Standing in the global spotlight she had humbled the Royal Family.' (Tom Bower, *Revenge,* p.380) The damage was done:

> Merely four years since their wedding the Sussexes had transformed the Royal Family from a relatively harmonious group, embracing multiculturalism as part of their service to Britain and the Commonwealth, into a beleaguered institution uncertain of its future. Single-handedly and for considerable financial gain, the Sussexes had tarnished the Queen's global reputation for unblemished decency. (Bower 411)

Thus, 'Harry's destiny was built on undermining the Windsors.' (Bower 389) Could it have been otherwise? Not really - he had too much rage in his soul.

Given the nonstop complaints from Meghan and Harry as regards how badly the British royal family treated them, let's put on record that Meghan Markle was given – a £32 million wedding, a £5 million house, £1 million on clothes, nine private holidays in 18 months, plus nannies, cooks, maids, P.A.'s, security, butlers, personal shoppers, a make-up and hair team, personal trainers whenever she wanted, access to world elites – and all she had to do was show up here and there and cut a few ribbons! *Ingratitude, thou marble-hearted fiend...*[56]

---

[54] A Scarsi, *Queen on the Brink: RF Faces Commonwealth Rebellion – Meghan Markle will spark Chaos'* Express 29.2.20.
[55] Lady C., M&H, p.7.
[56] Shakespeare, *King Lear 1,4.*

The Queen had firmly stated, "You can't be half-in, half-out" meaning that the couple had to decide, no longer could they drift around as semi-detached royals, turning up whenever they felt like it but not bound by burdensome commitments. A sense of duty and responsibility would be required. Years later, Palace officials queued up to tell their stories about being harassed and bullied by Meghan.

Figure: Harry is caught. A scene from the wedding of Princess Eugenie in 2018, which MM gatecrashed.

Harry's book *Spare* is dedicated to *Meg, Archie and Lily*, his fictional family. Harry received a twenty million advance for it. Holding its world No. 1 position on Amazon, it managed to garner an awesome one hundred thousand comments. Not only the dedication, but also in the acknowledgements at the end do his phantom kids appear: 'Above all my deepest and adoringest thanks to Archie and Lili, for letting papa go off to read and think and reflect...' I guess he needs to believe in them: *please, Archie and Lili, please exist!*

He's not a guy who would ever read a book, he prefers camping in Botswana where elephants and lions are a-roaming. If anyone wanted to do a portrait of Harry, I suggest it should be of him patting one of the lions in Botswana: a portrait of courage. The majesty of lions was traditionally an attribute of royalty.

Enchantment

Acting or LARPing doesn't seem quite adequate for Meghan's power, she does it so well that we could perhaps call it enchantment. It's January 2020 and she jets out to Canada, part of her process of pulling her prince out from England, far away from his RF. Why Canada, you may wonder, who wants to take a 10-month-old baby to Canada? We are shown her strolling through a wood, holding a rubber doll about two feet tall, clutching it round the neck with one arm, indicating that it is not too heavy, while she smiles at us.[57] Its left foot wobbles about, because it is made of rubber. A piece of cord around MM's neck holds up one of its arms. Surely this is a British royal prince, the very son of Prince Harry? Or at least it was a message to Harry that he'd better get himself over there to join her. His royal presence is necessary and he'd better be quick, to prevent the skeptical stories from breaking out.

Figure: the Duchess of Sussex holds a rubber doll: Vancouver, January 2020.

(We follow the insightful commentary from psychologist Emma Wells, 'TnT UK'). For much of 2019 Harry and Meghan could be seen to have a baby, however it seems that the real mother of the child decided that she wanted it back. After that the royal couple could not really hang around lacking a child. Harry is as it were imprisoned in the story and has no choice. That seems to have been what precipitated the move to Canada.

As to why the British media believed the fairy-tale, they had been sued and accused so often by Harry that they might have been reluctant to cast doubt over his paternity. But that doesn't quite seem adequate. Believing MMs play-acting is what gives her the power. Whether the Palace believed it or not – probably not – they were regrettably constrained by their protocols. One should not do this, or that – that is what trapped them, it

---

[57] TnT UK, *If this doesn't convince you, I don't know what will!* From 27 mins. SueMe '*Just Chattin' - Meghan & Her Archie Doll* ' at 10-20 mins.

was their undoing. Had they retained any decent Christian beliefs they would have realised that in this situation coming out with the truth was more important than anything else and was in fact the only thing that could have rescued them.

Again, we examine her power of fantasy. In the Royal Box in the Albert Hall on 16 January 2019, MM claims she was suicidal (for no reason) and that she sobbed her way through the concert, so Harry had to hold her hand and calm her down. She was then six months 'pregnant'. As Emma Wells a qualified psychotherapist points out, MM was 'glammed up' for this event and looked splendid in a blue sequin dress with no sign of any tears of distress – though Harry looked troubled. Did she have a 'kicking baby' inside her? Though pregnant with a royal she is claiming to be suicidal – why, Harry can hardly leave her alone in case she 'does it.' Admittedly she is in a stressful situation, of *pretending to be pregnant.* O, she's pregnant with a royal infant and taken to a marvellous concert where she'll sit in the royal box, with all the media flashbulbs going off around her, with Harry holding her hand, but she is so distressed, the poor girl! Then again after Archie's birth the blues returned: Harry in the Oprah interview recounted how returning from work in London he would find MM crying while breastfeeding Archie. Is it possible, for a woman to produce these two fluids at once?

The well-known British commentator Piers Morgan lost his job with ITV after waxing indignant about the Oprah interview, describing it as a 'diatribe of bilge … A two-hour Trashathon of our Royal Family.' Of MM he said, 'I don't believe a word she says. I wouldn't believe it if she read the weather report.'(Bower p375) Ofcom dismissed the 41,500 complaints it received in the wake of these comments saying Piers Morgan had a right to express his opinion. A lot of people agreed with him, and Oprah's credibility became severely undermined, for she had conducted that interview in a credulous and uncritical manner. Some comments were:

> "It was a disgusting interview. Oprah didn't ask any hard questions probably because she wasn't allowed to. I think this ruined her career. She was Markled!"

> "It wasn't an interview...it was a liar's whine fest."

"After the hatchet job, on the Royal Family, Oprah lost ALL credibility, in my opinion."

"Oprah was never a journalist. She was an entertainer. Why did anyone imagine she would ask interesting or pertinent questions? She allowed them to tell lies to the whole world. Weren't there around 17 lies officially documented at the end?"

After a month, the interview was deleted.

There could have been one especial moment, when the British people turned against Meghan. She and Harry were on a couch in their California home, making their long-winded Netflix series about being or not being a royal.[58] MM was scoffing at the way she had to curtsey to the Queen, waving her arms about to explain it. That Netflix program came out shortly after the death of England's Queen. The couple had been constantly griping about the RF not giving them enough of this and that. Her scoffing at that old British formality, a mere gesture of respect, was too much for many people. Mocking the newly-dead *for money* is not a way to make friends and influence people, especially not your own grandmother. Here are some comments:

- 'My disgust reached its peak when they both verbally abused a 96-year-old dying woman who was grieving the death of her husband of 70 years, in my mind both of them are abhorrent beyond words'

- This was the moment that finished it for me. The Queen had died 12 weeks before. I have never been more disgusted. And the other red line for me, was the outline of the recording device on her dress at the funeral and the spying of a tiny microphone attached to Harry's suit at the funeral. I was a bit sceptical to all the rumours until then, but when they were spotted and the looks of disgust on all his cousins and uncle and aunts, that finished me.

- For me, Meghan Markle's reputation crashed during her Oprah interview, her disrespect for, and spurious allegations against, the Royal Family, were all too abhorrent. Mocking her curtsey to the Queen confirmed my lack of respect, indeed dislike, for her.

---

[58] https://www.youtube.com/watch?v=pbn045a4f6g

- That clip is so disgusting. I was never a MM fan, but after watching that, she will never regain my respect. The Queen, in a way, was the world's grandmother. She was, and still is, much loved and respected by all. For MM to openly, purposely mock the Queen is a horrendous act of disrespect to the Queen, her family and the monarchy.

Harry just sat there, vaguely supporting his wife's theatrics. Shame upon you, Sir!

Piers Morgan denounced their Netflix series as 'Weapons-grade hypocrisy,' as 'a cynical attempt to manipulate viewers into questioning their own recollections of reality. A hundred million dollar whine-a-thon.. the truth doesn't really exist in their world ...its their truth . .nothing they ever say seems to stand up to reasonable scrutiny.. they have failed to provide a shred of evidence for their claims of racism.. their attempts to potentially bring down the British monarchy.' ('P. Morgan destroys H&M Netflix show')

Here are a couple of comments upon it:

- I haven't watched any trailers, or episodes….just the bits and pieces I see on different youtube channels is enough to make me feel abused by their horrendous rhetoric and outraged at their lies.

- Usually people that want to be free and have a private life don't do a Netflix series about their personal life and family drama...

The couple got into the list of the most disliked persons of 2024. The 'ginger and the whinger' had acquired a reputation of showing no respect for anybody. Invited to the coronation, Harry turned up and left ASAP while Meghan didn't even come. Considering that it was Charles who had escorted her down the aisle at her royal wedding people felt that was most disrespectful. Earlier, the couple had made it onto the cover of *Time* magazine's top People of the Year issue of 2021 with a heavily-photoshopped image of them looking like the best thing since John and Yoko. But how quickly did the goodwill fade …

Harry's army claims are what in the US army is called 'stolen valour', i.e. claiming to have done things that never happened. Such as being able to fly an Apache helicopter, which takes a year's hard training, to read all the complicated dials.[59] There are no pictures of him flying one. He was just given a photo-op sitting inside one, that is all. Likewise he sat on a practice firing range in front of a machine-gun, then lied in his book about killing 25 Taliban. Witnesses in the army in Afghanistan say he was never on the front line and would scoot off when any drug tests were being administered.

Here is an irate Emma Wells summarising the 'gaslighting of the public' by Harry, who 'has not really served on active duty:'

> He has not worked a day in his life…. He was not a pilot. He was called 'bunker Harry,' 'weekender Harry', because he turned up at weekends then went off again, was never on the front line, never in any danger, everything you saw was a photo-op, he disappeared when they had drug tests …

As to whether Harry is eligible to become a US citizen, he boasted in *Spare* about having taken cocaine, cannabis and mushrooms, probably why his visa application is currently (2024) being kept secret by the authorities. If he's lied in it in by denying this, he could face criminal charges. Many Americans are not happy with this privileged aristocrat getting the special treatment. His luxury home in California is next to several cannabis farms, which are perfectly legal, but they are exuding a strong stench.

Evicted from Invictus

Nigel Farage described Harry as a *treacherous little brat* after he was booed on the steps of St Paul's, for turning up there to mark the 10th anniversary of the Invictus games (April, 2024). That was after he and Meghan had returned from their quasi-royal tour of Nigeria, where *as if* he were a royal, he had inspected the guard, stood while God Save the King was played *and did not sing* - as if it were playing for him! He allowed himself to be addressed as 'your royal highness' and inspected schools … The couple had truly gone rogue. Using the brand name of the royals, it was said, they were watering down and muddying the brand. For their self-identity the two were clinging to a semblance of royalty, as if they could stay as non-working royals, doing exactly what they wanted with no sense

---

[59] The paragraph is based upon an account by an army veteran who served with Harry in Afghanistan: TnT UK 'WOW, confirmed its a lie! This goes deeper.' Harry passed thru Sandhurst though failing his exams, 8-20 mins.

of duty. They vowed to do more such tours and was this some plan to take over the Commonwealth? Harry had earlier been told firmly by the Queen that he could not be 'half-in, half-out', but now it seemed that he was doing just that. Meghan had rejoiced in some fifty different expensive costumes during the 3-day tour of a very poor country. She has a policy of never wearing the same dress twice, and let's not even think about how much that cost – or who pays it.

Soon, a couple of thousand veterans had quit the Invictus movement, being *fed up with the Harry and Meghan show.*[60]

A tour of Ghana was briefly announced, but what for? The Nigerian tour had ostensibly been to try and organise some Invictus games over there, however other co-organisers of the games were fairly livid at their quasi-royal theatrics (We're now in May, 2024). The President of Ghana declared that they would not be welcome, denouncing what he called their 'insincere activism efforts and self-promotion.' The people of Ghana did not wish to serve as accessories on their reality program, they had no interest in being part of some royal rehabilitation initiative. Soon H&M found themselves banned from the Invictus games, and for much the same reasons. The 'ginger and the whinger' were definitely not feeling appreciated.

Mike Tyndall, a former rugby player and husband of Princess Zara, became appointed as patron of Invictus games. He *banned* Harry from the 2024 Invictus Games, accusing him of 'a breach of the event's core values' and filed a lawsuit against the couple on the grounds that they had used the Invictus games for personal ventures. They had caused harmful delays, had embezzled funds and incurred financial losses as they exploited the movement for personal gain, misappropriating the charity's funds. The new CEO of Invictus agreed, putting out a statement that Harry would not be coming back anytime soon. Invictus veterans had been signing petitions objecting to MM turning up for the 2025 event.

The point of that Nigeria visit was, supposedly, to organise an Invictus-games event over there. People were relieved that Harry had something to do, some sense of purpose after he had chosen no longer to be royal. But after returning, he announced in a fit of pique that he would have to retire

---

[60] TnT UK , 'Tireless self-Service! 'Prince bunker harry what an absolute Joke'.

from the Invictus games. The reason? A few had booed him on the steps of St Paul's, as he arrived for a 10th anniversary memorial service of those games. That was a solemn occasion, when war-injured or damaged people from around the world were gathered and desiring to participate in these games – of which he'd been both a founder and a patron, ever since they started in 2014. His statement said:

> It is with a heavy heart that I have chosen to step away from this year's Invictus games. The mission and values of the Invictus games have always been dear to my heart. But I cannot in good conscience continue to be part of an event where my presence is so clearly unwanted.

People saw that as a betrayal. How could he be entrusted with anything in future if he thus acted in that peevish manner? They commented on how the couple had taken money out of the Invictus funding for their own expenses nor were they happy with the way in which he and Meghan were transforming the event into some sort of circus or fashion-display centred around them.

The 2025 games are due to be held in Vancouver, Canada. Canadians have been petitioning for removal of the duo from the Board of Directors. One comment ran:

> We welcome the athletes and their families in Vancouver without the horrible duo. That one's wife marching like a trollope in front of the British GB veterans was the last straw. Meghan should go back to working on the yachts or a strip club.

(Meghan had turned up and positioned herself at the front of a marching precession at the previous Invictus games, wearing a skimpy, unironed dress). It was noted that, in contrast, William had donated one million pounds to the Invictus funding without any flashy publicity. He'd won it from a newspaper as a lawsuit and he gave it all to the Invictus games.

Aftermath

The Queen's will has left a huge fortune to Charles, a hefty 110 million to 'Kate' in terms of jewellery and It has finally been determined that *not a penny* will go to Harry or Andrew. That is the price they pay for betraying the Firm. Harry had been behaving towards the royals as a one-man wrecking crew.

Liam, son of rock singer legend Rod Stewart, was getting married on a lovely summer afternoon in June in Croatia, however his blissful wedding was marred by Meghan Markle gatecrashing. The distinguished glitterati wedding guests were angry and jeered derisively at her, and soon a livid Sir Rod was yelling at her: "How dare you show your face here, you entitled lowlife! This is my son's special day, not your circus for attention-seeking!" Many a Briton would concur with that sentiment. Is she now estranged from Harry, people wondered?

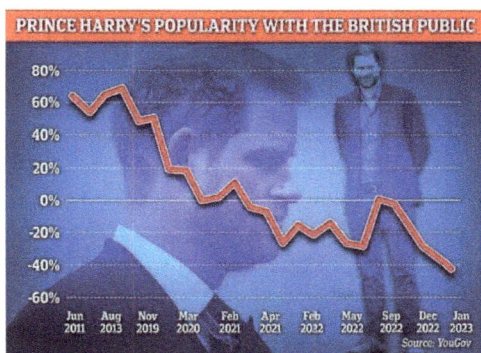

Figure: Harry's ever-descending popularity, since he married Meghan, 2011 - 2023. (YouGov Stats)

In June the British parliament debated the alleged children of Harry and Meghan: the couple had failed to provide any satisfactory proof of paternity for the two so it was decided to withdraw from them the titles of prince and princess. All of Harry's lame ducks were coming home to roost!

Many were calling for him to be stripped of his remaining royal title, but Charles is wary of doing that, partly because it would give the couple something else to complain about. But also, he and Harry well know that the latter has no royal blood. Were he put into a situation where he had nothing left to lose, he might just come out and say that, which would not do at all. The two are quasi-royals, more at home amongst the glamour and glitz of LA celebs than here in England.

Harry claims to be suffering from PTSD (post-traumatic stress disorder) and in his book acknowledges 'Special thanks to my UK therapist for helping to unravel years of unresolved trauma.' We now go back in time to the shattering and unresolved trauma which happened when he was only 13, which has to remain *the most formative thing* that ever happened to him and his brother. This royal story is like that of Henry VIII on steroids – bumping off a wife in order to acquire a new one.

Self-knowledge is a difficult thing, equally for us, the British people and for the two royal heirs in particular. Can the Windsor line endure, after so terrible an act?

Figure: What's left of the Windsors, after the Queen's departure. The lovely Kate is still there! Dracula-like, the figures cast no reflection in the mirror. Meghan proudly holds Harry's son Archie, though it is not hers.

Appendix

MI6 and Diana

'The most popular princess in the world had just been murdered by her own government - Her Majesty's Government.' [61]

Let us go through the bad memories one more time, of how the light of Princess Diana was extinguished. Our concern will be to highlight the role of MI6 and the Crown. We were all so badly misinformed following the crash, that it could be as well to clarify what happened and try to refute the false narrative.

It will probably be hard for the reader to appreciate, that the truth of this matter has only become resolved in the second decade of this 21st century.

Princess Diana had singlehandedly rescued the House of Windsor from being a dismal, unpopular relic from the past:

The face of this beautiful, uniquely popular woman dominated the front pages of every newspaper and magazine in the world for two decades and she was, had they possessed the common sense to recognise it, the jewel in the crown of the British royal family. [62]

She and Charles had very little in common. The show looked great, but that's all it was. As Botham well expressed the matter, Charles and Diana were 'two strangers locked in a masquerade of intimacy' (p.17).

A mere few years after their wedding, the phone lines of Buckingham Palace were being bugged. As early as 1985 they were being monitored by MI5 and Special Branch, without the royals being informed. Recordings were being sent to the NSA in America, with the full knowledge and connivance of prime Ministers John Major and Tony Blair. Diana was denounced as paranoid because she sensed that this was happening.

---

[61] John Morgan, *The Assassination of Princess Diana*, 2012, p.147.
[62] Noel Botham, *The Murder of Princess Diana*, 2007, p.xxiii

That wasn't all she was paranoid about. 'Diana lived constantly with the fear of being assassinated and put her thoughts in writing just one year before her death.' Why should the most famous woman in the world, so central to the British royal family, have such a fear?

Figure: Our Princess at her wedding, 1981

As the future king, Charles understood that he could not re-marry after divorcing Diana, or not so long as she was alive. He also grasped that, once his mother had passed away, popular pressure would grow for Diana to become the new Queen. Charles wished to marry Camilla and make her queen, but had no chance of that so long as Diana lived. There still lingered the effect of the tampax phone call scandal back in 1989, after which Camilla was receiving hate-mail by the sackload and could hardly venture out of her home. The royal family saw, ultimately, only one remedy.

Prince Philip had become vocal about the matter, thus a *Sunday Mirror* report on the threat he had made to Diana appeared *on the very morning* of her murder:

'He's been banging on about his contempt for Dodi and how he is undesirable as a future stepfather to William and Harry. Diana has been told in no uncertain terms about the consequences should she continue the relationship with the Fayed boy.'

This chapter has been guided by two excellent books, *The Murder of Princess Diana* by Noal Botham, 2007, and *Paris-London Connection, the Assassination of Princess Diana* by John Morgan, 2012. The latter summarises half a dozen bulky Diana-Inquest volumes which he composed, over 2008-12, an epic achievement. Only though it are we truly in a position to appreciate how, in fact, *MI6 did it, under instructions from the Crown.* Here are three evaluations of his work.

Sue Reid - Investigations Editor, Daily Mail, London: John Morgan's books lift the lid on the biggest scandal of our age. His perceptive forensic analysis of Princess Diana's death reveals an orchestrated cover-up by the British establishment, including powerful members of the judiciary, police, labour Government politicians and intelligence services. He shows that it was not a car accident caused by a drunken chauffeur that killed the royal icon: Diana was murdered in a clever plot to stop her marrying the playboy son of a Muslim Shop-keeper. As mother of William, the future king and head of the Church of England, she had to be stopped. And Morgan shows us how they did it, and then tried to hide the truth from the world – until he came along.

Michael Mansfield, QC, who served at the London Inquest: 'All of John Morgan's books are packed with the most incredible detail and the most careful analysis. He picks up the points that other authors have missed. He reaches compelling conclusions and offers telling comments. I have no doubt that the [Diana inquest] volumes written by John Morgan will come to be regarded as the 'Magnum Opus' on the crash... Of all the many books written about this case, Mr. Morgan's are by far the most detailed and analytical'.

Paul Sparks - UK journalist and film producer After the state-sponsored unlawful killing of Princess Diana, Dodi Fayed, and Henri Paul in 1997, the British and French authorities spent ten years in a cover up of what had taken place. When widespread public disquiet made further concealment impossible, they then held a six-month public inquest which gave the appearance of openness, but in reality sought to bury the truth beneath a vast and bewildering quantity of information, much of it irrelevant or misleading... In his series of books, John Morgan has performed an invaluable public service by organising this information into a systematic and comprehensible form... Morgan shows beyond all reasonable doubt how MI6 and the British Establishment (aided by members of French and US secret services) planned and executed the demise of a rebellious and troublesome princess. princessdianadeaththeevidence.weebly.com/the-reactuion.html

It concluded,

> Now the Royal Family may have decided it is time to settle up. (*Sunday Mirror* 31.8.97)

That meant exactly what it said! But how extraordinarily fateful that this should appear in print on that very morning. Does it not tell us, who did it?

In January 1997 Diana arrived in Angola and began her wonderful, in fact saintly, campaign to free the earth of landmines: a military weapon which continually targets and afflicts civilians, causing untold misery. A month later she received a phone call from Nicholas Soames, grandson of Winston Churchill, Minister of the Armed Forces, who had earlier averred on TV that Diana was 'in the advanced stages of paranoia.' She had been complaining that her rooms in the Palace were bugged, which turned out to be entirely correct. This time Soames tried to warn her off her landmine campaign with a death- threat: 'you never know when an accident is going to happen.' (Morgan, 38)

After that, in a speech (in June, to the Geographical Society) Di alluded to 'those ghastly Conservatives' – after which the Tories had no hope of beating Blair's New Labour! In her speech she asked, 'How can countries which manufacture and trade in these weapons square their conscience?' How touching, that she should think they have one.

In July of 1997 she and her two kids, 'the heir and the spare' as she called them, went on holiday in a luxury yacht belonging to Mohammed El Fayed, owner of *Harrods,* in the Mediterranean. There she met his son, Dodi. Synchronously, what was called the 'Way Ahead Group' at Buckingham Palace started to mull over the option of bumping her off. (Morgan, p.47) The British Crown has often been regarded as the cruellest, and maybe nothing has changed.

Around this time Di began to experience happiness, in contrast with the misery and torment she had experienced with the Windsors. Dodi and his father had been discussing with Diana the setting up of 'Diana Hospices' in relation to the victims of landmines. Upon arriving back in London, she wrote a thank-you for her week in France:

Thank you both so much for an enjoyable week in France. I cannot tell you how much I loved it ... We were given a wonderful and magical week and adored every minute of our stay ...William and

Harry and I had the best holiday imaginable and your family made us so welcome. (Morgan p.44)ff

The Queen chaired the Way Ahead Group, and in July of 1997 'the decision was made to assassinate Princess Diana outside of the UK.' It gave the nod to MI6 to go ahead. (Morgan, 48)[63] It had to happen abroad, where it would be easier to pretend that the law allowed such things – and harder to summon witnesses for any subsequent enquiry. As to how it would be done, the most plausibly deniable, tried-and-tested way was that of a car accident. MI6 would do it in conjunction with the CIA and the French intel agency DGSE.

The pre-prepared false narrative we were all given was simply:

- the driver Henri Paul was drunk,
- he was speeding, and
- the frenzied paparazzi by pursuing the car of Di and Dodi caused the crash in the Alma tunnel.
- She had forgotten to buckle up and so died.

None of those claims were true.

Years of research by John Morgan have produced what is surely the definitive, multi-volume study (2009-12) of the whole plot. He thereby drew the conclusion:

It is certainly MI6 that received the initial order to carry out the assassination and it was conducted under the MI6 umbrella. (p.13)

In Paris, the Alma tunnel lay conveniently close to El Fayed's Ritz hotel and Dodi Fayed's apartment. It was ideal for this black-op because its huge columns had no safety screens to stop cars hitting them. MI6's senior officer in France, Eugene Curley, received instructions about what had to happen – a complicated assassination plot to remove the most famous woman in the world - and he baulked, he wouldn't do it! He had to be

---

[63] July 1997 *Sunday Mirror* reported 'Top of the agenda at the forthcoming [Way Ahead Group] meeting is Diana.'

quickly replaced by Sherard Cowper-Coles, then based at MI6 in London. Also, Richard Spearman was sent over to Paris to assist him, arriving on August 26th, mere days before the event. Of the various MI6 operatives stationed in Paris,

> '... only two or three –probably Cowper-Coles, Caton and Spearman – would have known ahead of time the precise goal of the operation. The operation required some five experienced, proficient riders on motorbikes, a driver and car that would wait near the tunnel ahead of the incident, and a couple of ambulance-based doctors 'for a back-up plan in case Diana survived.' (Morgan 54)

It was planned down to the last detail.

Timing was crucial, mainly because the US President, charmed by Di, had announced that he would support an international ban on landmines, due to be ratified on September 16th. As Jerry White, co-founder of 'Land Mine Survivors Network' said, "Princess Di can be very proud. She was central to pushing Clinton off the fence." A worldwide ban on landmines! Once Clinton announced that decision, on 18th August, it was all systems go.

Furthermore, Di was evidently pregnant. Had the news been allowed to emerge that she had become pregnant from a Muslim, who had given her a gold engagement ring, and that she was blissfully happy for the first time ever – well, all ~~hell~~ heaven might break loose! She had to be bumped off before all that, which would have changed the world we live in.

Only days before her last trip with Dodi, Di went into a London hospital, to undergo a pregnancy scan (Botham, pxxxii). In August 1997, a boat carrying Di and Dodi landed in Monaco, so that the happy couple could go into town and choose a gold engagement ring, from the romantic *Dis-moi-Oui* range ('tell me yes'). A week later they purchased that very ring in Paris, a mere couple of hours before their death. That final visit to Paris was in order to collect that engagement ring.

Once the car and the short route that it would take through Paris to Dodi's apartment had been finalised, a specialist intelligence team set to work on the rear seat belts, to ensure that they would not work.

MI6 and Diana

Henri Paul as overseer of security in the Paris Ritz hotel was working for MI6 and probably the French intel services as well. As British MI6-defector Richard Tomlinson stated:

> The acting chief of security at the Ritz Hotel, Henri Paul, had been working for the British secret service for years. I came across his personal file when I was working for them in 1993. Henri Paul was a long-standing agent. (Botham 127)

He was found to have huge amounts of cash stashed in various bank accounts – paid in bank drafts originating in London, almost certainly from the MI6 paymaster's office. He wasn't due to be at work that day. That night, persons close to him noticed no whiff of alcohol in his breath. When they drove off he took the car on a diversion from its intended route so that it could go into the *Pons D'Alma* tunnel. He was not speeding, just driving at a steady 65 km/hr as recorded by the speed cameras. The couple were doing a late-night trip after dinner, which was ideal for MI6's purpose, being under cover of darkness. Clearly he didn't know the plan, which involved his own death.

A swarm of paparazzi were following half a mile behind them, hardly a nuisance. Whereas, that afternoon and evening a swarm of MI6 *fake* paparazzi on motorbikes had been pursuing Diana and Dodi, in order to give the impression of being dangerous, so as to facilitate the later pinning of blame upon them. The bodyguard Trevor Rees-jones later wrote of these that 'they [Diana and Dodi] were surrounded by screaming motorcycles, darting around the target vehicles, sometimes two to a bike.'

James Andanson, driver of an old white Fiat Uno, caused the crash. He was 'a member of the UKN, a small corps of part-time British Secret Intelligence Service agents who provide miscellaneous services to MI6 such as surveillance and photographic expertise.' (Botham 221). The whole thing was synchronised so that he would be hanging around at the entrance of the tunnel just as the Mercedes carrying Dodi, Diana, Henri-Paul and Rees-Jones entered it (The latter survived but had a memory wipeout). Andanson had to swerve over so his car just scraped its front, causing it to veer off course. At that instant the passenger on the motor-cycle in front of them beamed a brilliant flash of light into the driver's eyes which instantly blocked his mind and vision, causing the crash to happen.

French officials strenuously denied any of this and it took years for the truth to emerge. According to one of Andanson's neighbours, 'he boasted openly of not only having been in Paris, but present at the moment when Diana was killed.' (Botham 227, Morgan 123) That could have been unwise because he died in an horrific 'suicide' a few years later, burnt up inside his car. Some people just can't keep a secret.

That key character, Andanson, was not identified by the French police but by the private investigation conducted by Al Fayed. That was not surprising, since 'French Intelligence refused to release any information from their files on Henri Paul and James Andanson – both of whom worked for the French secret service.' (Botham, p.xxiii) In the meantime the true assassins – the motorbike riders and the ambulance doctors – remain free (Morgan, p.124).

Mi5 whistleblower David Shayler commented thus upon the *modus operandi:*

> The white Fiat was traced to James Andanson. Other paparazzi have reported his connections to MI6, which has a long record of using journalists and photographers as agents. When interviewed by police, Andanson claimed not to be in Paris that night. Yet forensics indicated that the Fiat had been in the tunnel and had been sold after the crash.

> It is far more likely that the crash was the work of MI6 agents – as opposed to serving officers. Known as 'surrogates' or 'cut-offs', they are otherwise unconnected to the service so MI6 can drop the operation should the agents be caught. As part of the recruitment, agents are asked if they are prepared to be 'ethically flexible.' If the answer is no they are not recruited. (Botham p230)

But, do the British people want their intel service to employ 'ethically flexible' killers? Do they want all this cloak-and-dagger skullduggery going on? To quote Shayler one more time:

> Vehicle "accidents" are used as a way of assassination precisely because they are such a common cause of death. It is easy for the authorities to claim that anyone crying foul play is simply a "conspiracy theorist."

MI6 was quite used to arranging such operations at short notice, as former MI6 agent Richard Tomlinson has explained. It had earlier devised an identical assassination plot for the Serbian president Milosevic in 1992 – on his way into a tunnel with blinding strobe light. It was a *readily-deniable* technique. "Everything had happened exactly as specified in the MI6 plan to kill Slobodan Milosevic" said Tomlinson.[64] He added that, an unusually large number of his former colleagues were in Paris that night.

The crash happened at 12.23 am, after which Diana was heard repeating 'My God, my God.' She was suffering from internal bleeding and, experts have stated, could have been rescued. An ultra-slow ambulance took 17 minutes to arrive, from 2 kilometers away. At 12.40 she was lifted into it, after which it crept along taking a quite incredible *hour and a half* to reach the hospital. Author John Morgan commented upon the behaviour of the doctor in the ambulance, Jean-Marc Martino:

'Martino, had he been interested in saving Diana, would have been trying to get her to a hospital as soon as possible. Yet that is not what occurred. Diana didn't arrive at the La Pitié – *Salpêtrière* Hospital until 2.06 am. Her heart stopped beating minutes later. (Morgan, p.99)

The ambulance doctor did, in effect, kill her. At the hospital, the senior doctor on duty grew suspicious about what had happened because the delay of that ambulance made no sense to him. In completing her death certificate he ticked the box 'Yes' for 'suspicious death.'

It would soon be alleged that the driver Henri-Paul was drunk, by pretending to find high alcohol in his blood: a blood sample from his corpse was swapped over with that of a drunk who had also died that night. The latter turned out to be a suicide who had gassed himself, so that his blood had not only to high levels of alcohol but also very high carbon monoxide, which the authorities tried to keep quiet about. The high CO_2 found in the blood remained a major flaw in the official cover-up and in fact demonstrated that it could not have been Henri-Paul's blood.

Within an hour of the crash, the authorities started blaming the paparazzi. Blame is cast upon an innocent third party – that is a central

---

[64] dailymail.co.uk/news/article-517115/The-MI6-plots-assassinate-Milosevic-were.html

feature of state-fabricated terror and it has to happen *before* the police have started to investigate the matter. In fact, paparazzi were absent when the car crashed. With one accord the media were soon braying that it was an accident and not planned in any way. Early the next morning the Alma tunnel was swept clean and re-opened for traffic, which clearly suggests a cover-up. The company Mercedes-Benz offered their expert assistance in examining the wrecked car, but the French authorities declined – after all, they already knew it was an accident.

A decision was made to partially embalm the body with formaldehyde, a procedure which would corrupt any toxicology test and spoil the determination of possible pregnancy. The order seems to have come from a UK source, being relayed by Sir Michael Jay, the British ambassador in Paris, on behalf of Prince Charles' St James Street office. It didn't come from Diana's next of kin and so was illegal under French law. Why would a French hospital accept an order from a foreign power as regards post-mortem procedure? A radiologist who examined X-ray photos of Diana's internal organs told friends that "she saw a small foetus, of probably six to ten weeks, clearly visible in the princess' womb.' (Botham p.192)

Two professional photographers in London had managed to acquire high-value photos of the crash. The very day after, within 24 hours of the crash, their homes were burgled. No silver or credit cards or expensive cameras etc. were removed – only, all the hard drives and computer files of the terrible images were taken. (Botham, p.290). That has to be a British intel job, done with lightning speed, pointing unequivocally to the perpetrators of the operation.

The Queen's coroner John Burton was soon able to gain control over the post-mortem and he for long managed to block any subsequent Inquest. In 2001 he told the *Daily Telegraph* that an inquest into Diana and Dodi's deaths would be "a waste of everyone's time and money" and he campaigned for a change in the law so that no inquiry would have to be held! (Botham, p.151-2) However pressure built up after Diana's butler Paul Burell published a handwritten note by Diana about how her husband was plotting to have her removed in a car-crash.[65] After huge public demand an inquest finally began in January of 2007, with Scotland Yard commissioner Lord Stevens heading the investigation:

Scotland Yard would have to create a perception that the deaths were being fully investigated, when actually what was to occur was possibly the biggest cover-up the British police had ever been involved in. (Morgan, p.147)

Diana's tomb or burial-place had to be hidden away. Greatly did the royals fear lest it became a place of pilgrimage for the British people, had it been visible somewhere. The last thing they wanted was such a tribute to Our Princess. Instead she was buried on an island surrounded by a lake on the Spencer Estate. Now and then it opens to the public – for a fee.

> *Beautiful must be the mountains whence ye come,*
> *And bright in the fruitful valleys the streams, wherefrom*
> *Ye learn your song:*
> *Where are those starry woods? O might I wander there,*
> *Among the flowers, which in that heavenly air*
> *Bloom the year long!*
>
> *Nay, barren are those mountains and spent the streams:*
> *Our song is the voice of desire, that haunts our dreams,*
> *A throe of the heart,*
> *Whose pining visions dim, forbidden hopes profound,*
> *No dying cadence nor long sigh can sound,*
> *For all our art.*

Robert Bridges *Nightingale*

---

[65] Paul Burrell had it published in the *Mirror* (20.10.03), blanking out the name of the person whom she believed was plotting her murder: which was of course Charles. See Youtube, 'Did Princess Diana Predict Her Death?' (8m. views)

Appendix 2   Royal blood

Is there some mystique to the *sangreal*, the *sang-royale*, the royal blood? Both sides of the British royal family – that of the Queen and of the Duke of Edinburgh - show high-level Nazi connections, both having had contact with Adolf Hitler and various people under him. The history has been deleted here, and we have little more than old photographs that somehow could not be lost being already in the public domain.

Prince Philip came from a family of high-ranking Nazis. His mother Princess Alice of Battenburg was born to Prince Louis of Battenberg and Princess Victoria of Hesse-by-Rhine, both from central Germany. Phillip was the Duke of Schleswig-Holstein-Sonderburg-Glücksburg. He is pictured attending the funeral in Nazi Germany of his elder sister Cecile as a 16-year-old schoolboy in 1937, flanked by other relatives who were dressed in SS and Brown-shirt uniforms. The Queen later learned how 'her marriage was almost scuppered by Philip's links to one of Hitler's closest henchmen.'[66] A photo shows Prince Philip's sister Princess Sophie sitting opposite Hitler at the 1935 wedding of Hermann Goering.[67] His three sisters married German princes who became leading Nazis. The child-queen Elizabeth was taught to make the Nazi salute by her father George VI (who met Hitler) in 1933, in the gardens of Balmoral, shown in a photo published by *The Sun* (18.7.15).

The briefly-ruling Edward VIII was brother of George VI and thus the Queen's uncle. He had pro-German sympathies and believed that there was no need for a war between England and Germany, so he had to go. Hitler tried to arrange a marriage between him and a German aristocrat, to cement Anglo-German friendship but it didn't work. He preferred a twice-divorced American woman. After the war, efforts were made to lose what

---

[66]   constantinereport.com/prince-philip-pictured-at-nazi-funeralthe-nazi-relative-that-the-royals-disowned
[67]   aanirfan.blogspot.com/2017

was called the 'Windsor File,' i.e. documents showing friendship of the Windsors with Nazis.[68]

William has the once-and-future king aura, having got himself born smack on the summer solstice, thanks to an induced birth by Diana, right after a solar eclipse. Whatever his future may be, one should not altogether ignore his German and National-Socialist ancestry.

Via his Spencer blood, William will be the first of King Charles II's lineage to ascend the throne, since the Merry Monarch himself.

---

[68] Andrew Morton, *17 Carnations, the Windsors, the Nazis and the Cover-up* 2015.

Index